TWAYNE'S WORLD AUTHORS SERIES

A Survey of the World's Literature

Sylvia E. Bowman, Indiana University

GENERAL EDITOR

SPAIN

Gerald Wade, Vanderbilt University
Janet Díaz, University of North Carolina, Chapel Hill

EDITORS

Contemporary Spanish Poetry (1898 - 1963)

TWAS 373

CONTEMPORARY SPANISH POETRY (1898 - 1963)

By CARL W. COBB
University of Tennessee

TWAYNE PUBLISHERS

A DIVISION OF G. K. HALL & CO., BOSTON

Library of Congress Cataloging in Publication Data

Cobb, Carl W.
  Contemporary Spanish poetry (1898 - 1963).

  (Twayne's world authors series ; TWAS 373 :
Spain)
  Bibliography: p. 152 - 57.
  Includes index.
  1. Spanish poetry — 20th century — History and
criticism.   I. Title.
PQ6085.C56   1976   861'.6'209   75-23016
ISBN 0-8057-6202-7

MANUFACTURED IN THE UNITED STATES OF AMERICA

For Jane,
 in growing faith.

Contents

About the Author

Carl W. Cobb, after receiving two degrees from Peabody College, earned his doctorate at Tulane University in 1961. He also studied in Mexico City and at the Universidad Nacional in Columbia, and he spent the summer of 1968 in Spain doing research. In addition to publishing articles in the *Philological Quarterly* and the *Revista de estudios hispánicos,* he is the author of the Twayne World Authors Series volumes on *Federico García Lorca* (1967) and *Antonio Machado* (1971), both of which have been well received by the critics. At present, Dr. Cobb is a Professor of Spanish at the University of Tennessee in Knoxville. As a graduate professor, his areas of specialization are Modern Spanish literature and Spanish poetry.

Preface

In the twentieth century, Spanish literature has enjoyed a rebirth of such proportions that already the major critics have guardedly begun to characterize the period as a second Golden Age. The first Golden Age, which spanned the years from 1492 until around 1650, was the age of Ferdinand and Isabella, Charles V, and Philip II; of Columbus, Cortez, and Pizarro; of the dramatists Lope de Vega, Calderón, and Tirso de Molina; of the mystics St. John of the Cross, St. Theresa, and Fray Luis de León; of the picaresque novel and the immortal Cervantes. Moreover, during this great age there was an outstanding group of major poets: Garcilaso de la Vega, Fernando de Herrera, St. John of the Cross, Lope de Vega, Luis de Góngora, and Francisco de Quevedo. During the Golden Age, Spain was of course at the forefront of the European scene, not only in literature but also in politics. This possible second Golden Age, which in totality must remain inferior to the first, is all the more remarkable when we consider that Spain has recovered almost none of her former political prestige, and therefore the renaissance has been completely literary.

For the purposes of this study, it is important to emphasize that the major achievement in this renaissance of the twentieth century has been in the area of lyric poetry. In a short but profound article the critic Pedro Salinas argued convincingly that the "sign" of twentieth-century Spanish literature is *lyric*, that even prose writers such as Valle-Inclán and Azorín wrote lyrically.[1] In his important book on modern European poetry, Hugo Friedrich declares: "From the beginning of the 20th century there has flourished in Spain a poetry of such abundance and quality that the critics of the country speak of a second Golden Age in their literature, and the foreign critics see themselves obliged to admit they are right."[2] He adds that the poetry of Antonio Machado, Jiménez, Lorca, Vicente Aleixandre, Jorge Guillén, Rafael Alberti, Luis Cernuda, and others is perhaps the best in modern European literature. This conclusion is especially significant when we consider that, because of Spain's social and political traditionalism (called by some backwardness) in relation to the rest of Europe, there has developed a certain prejudice against Spanish authors.

In approaching the poets and poetry of the twentieth century, especially those of the Generation of '98, we must attempt to clarify a confusing problem bequeathed to us by zealous literary historians. Toward 1900 two recognizable movements arose in the Hispanic countries. The *Modernismo* of Rubén Darío, which began in Hispanic America, followed the aesthetic emphases of the nineteenth-century current initiated by Edgar Allan Poe and developed in France by Baudelaire, Verlaine, Mallarmé, and Rimbaud. In Spain, the movement associated with the Generation of '98, led by Unamuno and Angel Ganivet, developed the theme (often called the Castilian theme) of the analysis and regeneration of Spain's cultural traditions. Thus, while the term "Generation of '98" would seem to embrace this whole generation of Spanish authors, in critical practice only those who pursued the Castilian theme were considered a part of it. The Spanish literary historians have had a field day placing writers in either *Modernismo* or the Generation of '98, but unfortunately no two have ever agreed upon the members of each group. For our purposes, an acute problem has been the classification of the great poet Juan Ramón Jiménez, who has generally been excluded from the Generation of '98 because he ignored the Castilian theme.

In later years, Jiménez himself spearheaded the attempt to establish a broader philosophical base for modern Spanish literature. In fact, the critic Federico de Onís had earlier formulated a general definition of "modernism" acceptable to Jiménez: "Modernism is the Hispanic form of the universal crisis in letters and in spirit which around 1885 . . . was manifested in art, science, religion, and politics. . . ."[3] For Jiménez, modernism in Spain was established primarily by two great "revolutionaries": Unamuno, who represented metaphysical freedom, and Darío, who represented aesthetic freedom.[4] Recent critics such as Ricardo Gullón have accepted and defended this broader definition of modernism as developed by Onís and Jiménez. Therefore we prefer to consider Jiménez and all the authors of his time as belonging to the Generation of '98, and we shall treat Darío's *Modernismo* and the Castilian theme in a specific context. The general movement which Jiménez called merely "modern" embraces all the poets of the twentieth century, despite certain differences of emphasis and manner in their poetry.

The development of such a vast subject as Spanish poetry of the twentieth century offers very difficult problems of organization, selection, and treatment. In fact, even the major Spanish critics have lacked the nerve to attack this subject. The dean of Spanish critics, Don Dámaso Alonso, has offered a *Poesía española contemporánea*, but it is only a collection of articles, some of them minor. José Luis Cano's *Poesía española del siglo XX* falls into the same category. The poet Luis Cernuda's *Estudios sobre poesía española contemporánea* develops an overview of the period with many insights, but his critical discussions are too personal and incomplete. In her two books, Concha Zardoya presents excellent critical studies of important themes in the major poets, but without attempting to treat the entire period. Indeed, the only book embracing twentieth-century Spanish poetry is Gustav Siebenmann's *Die moderne Lyrik in Spanien*, which develops major themes.

Thus lacking an authoritative model, we have decided after much soul-searching to develop our study by concentrating upon the work of a limited number of major poets. These will include Miguel de Unamuno (whose importance as a cultural figure has at times overshadowed his poetry), Antonio Machado, and Juan Ramón Jiménez of the Generation of '98. Of the Generation of '27, we are giving special importance to Federico García Lorca, Jorge Guillén, and Vicente Aleixandre, with reduced but significant space to Pedro Salinas, Gerardo Diego, Rafael Alberti, and Luis Cernuda. The poets since 1939 are treated only briefly, since most of them have not finished their careers. Sainz de Robles' extensive *Antología de la poesía española* and various literary histories demonstrate the ineffectiveness of presenting an interminable selection of poets with only a few pages of critical discussion and scattered selections from each. Our discussion of only a limited number of poets of course involves the serious problem of selection, and we shall surely be unjust to many important poets.

At the same time that we provide historical background on the poetry, we have chosen to treat the central themes and poems of each poet in greater depth than is usual in such a book as this. We therefore trust we have presented more of a critical analysis than a history of each poet's work. This naturally involves the insoluble problem of providing adequate translations. Since we have received some commendation for our translations of Lorca and Machado in our earlier Twayne books, we shall attempt to provide our own poetic translations, because few adequate ones exist for the poets studied. Of course, in translation we cannot demonstrate the marvelous technical achievements of most of these poets, since great modern poets are inevitably wedded to their language.

While the problems of developing a book on the Spanish poets of the twentieth century are clearly formidable, certainly the times are propitious for us to confront the task. At the present moment in liberal arts, there is an intensifying interest in approaching the literature of other cultures in translation. On major university campuses, language departments, in addition to traditional language teaching, are attempting to provide classes in translation in French, Germanic, and Hispanic culture, as well as many others. We are certain that the major poets we have selected are worthy of serious study. In Spain and elsewhere competent critics have already established their worth, and in English various individual poets, especially Jiménez, Lorca, Guillén, and Cernuda, have stimulated books of translation and criticism. We trust that this Twayne book will provide a useful introduction to a fruitful period in Spanish literature.

Acknowledgments

Señor Francisco H. Pinzón Jiménez has graciously given his permission to quote from the poetry of Juan Ramón Jiménez.

I am grateful to Janet Levy-Feigenbaum, who patiently typed and retyped the manuscript; and to my friend Yulan M. Washburn for his continuing encouragement and critical suggestions.

Chronology

1895   Unamuno (born 1864) publishes his essay *En torno al casticismo* (Concerning the Essential Spanish Character).

1896   Publication of Rubén Darío's *Prosas profanas*.

1898   Spanish American War, the event celebrated in the term "Generation of '98."

1903   Jiménez (born 1881) publishes his *Arias tristes* (Sad Arias); Antonio Machado publishes his *Soledades* (Solitudes), second edition in 1907.

1905   Publication of Darío's *Cantos de vida y esperanza*.

1911   Publication of Unamuno's *Rosario de sonetos líricos* (Rosary of Lyric Sonnets).

1912   First edition of Machado's *Campos de Castilla* (Fields of Castile).

1916   Publication of Jiménez's *Diario de un poeta reciencasado* (Diary of a Newly Married Poet).

1918 -   The development of ultraism in Spanish poetry.
1923

1922   Gerardo Diego publishes *Imagen* (Image).

1923   Publication of Pedro Salinas' *Presagios* (Presages).

1925   Rafael Alberti publishes *Marinero en tierra* (Sailor Ashore).

1927   Celebration of Góngora Tricentennial, the event celebrated in the term "Generation of '27."

1928   Publication of Federico García Lorca's *Romancero gitano* (Gypsy Ballads), the first edition of Jorge Guillén's *Cántico* (Canticle), and Vicente Aleixandre's first book, *Ámbito* (Ambit).

1928 -   The development of surrealism in Spanish poetry.
1936

1929   Publication of Alberti's *Sobre los ángeles* (*Concerning the Angels*).

1935   Aleixandre publishes *La destrucción o el amor* (Destruction or Love).

1936   Spanish Civil War begins; publication of Luis Cernuda's *La realidad y el deseo* (Reality and Desire); and Jiménez's *La estación total* (The Total Season).

1940   Publication of Lorca's *Poeta en Nueva York (Poet in New York)* in Mexico.

1941   Diego publishes *Alondra de verdad* (Lark of Truth).

1944   Publication of Dámaso Alonso's *Hijos de la ira (Children of Wrath)*.

1949   Jiménez publishes *Animal de fondo* (Animal of Depth).

1950 - The development of poetry of human solidarity and com-
1963   munication.

1963   Beginning of a poetry influenced by the mass media.

CHAPTER 1

Backgrounds of Twentieth-Century Spanish Poetry

THE literary generation later called the Generation of '98 inherited a depressing historical and cultural situation. From her point of maximum influence in the Golden Age, Spain's fortunes in the Western world had gradually suffered a decline of centuries, the final blow being the brief but disastrous Spanish American War of 1898. Stimulated by an awareness of the crisis besetting Spanish culture, this group — which includes Unamuno, Angel Ganivet, Pío Baroja, Azorín, Ramón del Valle-Inclán, Manuel and Antonio Machado, and Jiménez — set out to renovate Spain, Spanish literature, and at times even themselves. These figures, led by Unamuno, generally felt the attraction of two strong but opposing currents. On the one hand, they were attracted to Spain's glorious past, and naturally set out to explore Spanish culture, history, and landscape in order to discover the reasons for Spain's past successes, so that they could utilize their discoveries in determining a better future. On the other hand, they turned toward the ideas and culture of Europe, with the aim of "Europeanizing," or modernizing, Spain. Finally Unamuno came to represent the defenders of Spanish culture, while Ortega y Gasset became the spokesman for Europeanization. Even a supposed traditionalist like Unamuno, however, was heavily influenced by the philosophical currents outside Spain.

Whereas previously the Spaniards had clung to their traditionalist Catholic culture, during the latter half of the nineteenth century a flood of European ideas began to inundate Spain. Luis Granjel in his *Panorama de la Generación del 98* devotes many dense pages to the profusion of thinking and ideas which began to penetrate into Spain. The political ideas of Marx's *Communist Manifesto* made converts of a few Spaniards, who developed isolated pockets of anarchy and preached class struggle. The effect of the ideas of Darwinism was to challenge the traditional bases of life as moral and religious. The philosophy of Schopenhauer, especially his emphasis upon the will (or drives) and his pessimism, aroused consternation in Spain. The ideas of Nietzsche, specifically his attacks on Christianity and his projection of the superman were partially rejected in horror and then more or less assimilated as a new and daring individuality. Unamuno in particular discovered the "agonizing" Christianity of the Dane Kierkegaard. From the movements of symbolism and decadentism the poets in particular received the lesson that the artist must work outside his decaying culture, and often in rebellion against it. Around the turn of the century, Bergson's ideas of time and the importance of intuition stimulated serious interest, especially in Antonio Machado.

From this profusion of ideas, some modern, some ancient, the figures of the early twentieth century were searching desperately for a viable philosophy. As Unamuno and Machado comprehended clearly, the two great currents in Western culture had run aground: the tradition of Christianity and the tradition of rationalism, which gradually undermined the Christian faith during the centuries of the Renaissance and the Enlightenment. While the cultural figures in the rest of Europe had been gradually prepared for this shock, in Spain Unamuno's generation suddenly found itself without the safe moorings of the Catholic faith. We must emphasize that this shock of a whole generation's finding itself rootless was the stimulus for its personal and literary achievement. Each figure set out to make his own world from the parts of previous tradition he found viable.

In addition to the influx of European ideas, a peculiar but significant movement called *Krausismo* or *Krausism* developed inside Spain toward the end of the century.[1] Based upon the philosophy of a minor nineteenth century German thinker named Christian F. Krause, this movement was initiated in Spain by Sanz del Río after 1850 and developed into an educational system by Francisco Giner (1839 - 1915), who founded the Institución Libre de Enseñanza in 1876, that is, free (*libre*) from the influence of both church and state. The Free Institute proposed to provide for its students a harmonious education, a total development of the personality, which would combine the cultivation of sensitivity and artistic taste, preparation for a profession, spiritual education, and an austere moral sense of life. The Krausists believed in the perfectibility of man, social progress, and the essential beauty of life. If this program seems bland and general, in practice it proved to be fiercely revolutionary.

The followers of Krausism bitterly rejected the Catholic church and its hierarchy and sought to bypass the church in all its programs. Surely Antonio Machado is the outstanding model of *Krausismo* in Spain. He sought the total development of the individual, and himself exemplified the austere moral sense. And, somewhat paradoxically, he was "Christian" in his belief in the brotherhood of man and emphasis upon moral values, but he was intransigent in rejecting the Catholic church as an institution.

There is complete agreement that lyric poetry was in a state of utter stagnation by 1898. The three poets widely popular in the last half of the nineteenth century had finished their careers and become targets of sweeping criticism. Núñez de Arce represented the grandiloquent voice and the public stance; José Zorrilla exemplified a superficial type of Romantic poetry; Ramón de Campoamor devoted himself to a manner of ironic skepticism which the next generation found common and trite. However, two other poets of the nineteenth century have since been revived by the poets of our century, although both of them had disappeared from the scene by 1885. During his short lifetime, the Sevillian poet Gustavo Adolfo Bécquer (1836 - 1870) worked in isolation, since his intimate lyric manner was opposed to the prevailing mode of stridency and grandiloquence. Although a major critic of his time airily dismissed his poetry as "Nordic sighs," Bécquer has turned out to be the only nineteenth-century poet revered by those of this century; indeed, he is now considered the first modern poet in Spain. His brief *Rimas*, unpublished at his death in 1870, has received extensive critical attention and appreciation. Although of lesser importance, the Galician poetess Rosalía de Castro (who died in 1885) succeeded in a few lyrics in reaching a quality of intimacy which has touched later poets, such as Machado and Cernuda. Around 1890, then, the eminent critic Clarín lamented that the older poets were gone and that the new generation was "sickly, lazy, and without ideals." And he concluded rhetorically: "How is a new poetry going to come out of all this?"[2]

The answer to Clarín's plaintive question appeared almost as if by miracle in the person of the great Nicaraguan poet Rubén Darío. In 1899, with his reputation firmly consecrated by the publication of *Prosas Profanas* in 1896, Darío made a second visit to Spain and established permanent contact with Unamuno, Jiménez, and Antonio Machado. Darío represented the new and dazzling movement of *Modernismo,* and it is difficult for us today to understand the un-

bridled enthusiasm with which the literary figures in both Spain and
Hispanic America reacted to Darío and *Modernismo*. Typical is the
youthful outburst of Jiménez in his journal *Helios* in 1902: "This
modern maestro is genial, is great, is intimate, is exquisite, is
tormented, is diamantine."[3]

Darío's *Modernismo* in this phase is essentially a movement in
which the poet retreats from the workaday world and retires to his
"ivory tower" so that he may become a creator of beauty, sensuous
beauty. His poetry is aristocratic, sensual, plastic, exotic, musical,
and sonorous. Darío is usually given sweeping credit for renovating
the technical forms of poetry in the period of *Modernismo*. He
revived the six-syllable line of the medieval popular song, the rare
enneasyllable, the decasyllable, the traditional hendecasyllable with
unconventional accents, the balanced twelve-syllable line called *arte
mayor*, the medieval Alexandrine, and even the hexameter, known
to Americans through Longfellow's *Evangeline*. Darío's poetry in
this period represents the triumph of the aesthetic over moral and
social values.

But it is unjust to Darío (as was Unamuno, for example) not to
emphasize that in his second period he employed his talents in
creating a poetry of human, social, and historical values. Driven by
growing personal concerns and stimulated by his official travels, the
poet abandoned his exoticism and turned toward the twin themes of
his own destiny and that of the Spanish-speaking peoples. His other
great book of poetry, *Cantos de vida y esperanza* (Songs of Life and
Hope), published in 1905, clearly emphasizes the brotherhood of the
Spanish-speaking peoples. In individual poems he returns to important Spanish cultural figures, such as Góngora, the painter Velázquez, and Cervantes. The three Spaniards destined to become the
major poets of the Generation of '98 — Unamuno, Jiménez, and Antonio Machado — initially reacted very strongly to Darío's influence, though gradually each one assimilated, modified, or rejected this influence and developed his own style.

Certain other poets of this generation, destined to become minor
ones, continued to develop the manner of Darío, each with his own
specific themes. A special case is that of the Andalusian Salvador
Rueda (1857 - 1933). Even before meeting Darío, Rueda had
already achieved certain innovations in his poetry with his ex-
periments in form and his projection of erotic vitality. Initially impressed with Rueda's potential, Darío later became his literary
enemy when he published the remark that Rueda was not progress-

ing in his poetry. In fact, only in his later poems, where everyone assumes he was imitating Darío, does Rueda achieve an excellence in the *modernista* manner, such as his Alexandrine sonnet "Arch of Triumph." Actually Salvador Rueda merits only a minor position as a precursor of modern poetry, for his very fecundity, his lack of concentration and organization of theme, proved his undoing.

Another minor poet but a major literary figure was Ramón del Valle-Inclán (1866 - 1936), who declared himself a disciple of Darío. While he earned his literary reputation as a writer of aesthetic prose, Valle-Inclán's achievement in lyric poetry is solid and original, although of limited quantity. Impressed with Darío's exoticism, Valle-Inclán discovered a kind of exoticism in the religious traditions of his native Galicia. In his *Aromas de leyendas,* he is concerned, not with the religious, but with the aesthetic and sensuous effects of the Catholic ritual and traditions. In his final book of poetry, *La pipa de Kif* (The Marijuana Pipe), Valle-Inclán turns his former aesthetic manner inside out, creating not beauty but ugliness, in a world of turbulence, violence, and defamation. These verses are "funambulesque" and "grotesque"; the poet's scene becomes the tavern, the carnival, and even the zoo. Although in a popular form, these poems reveal Valle-Inclán's continuing preoccupations with the aesthetic aspects of poetry.

As a final representative of Darío's modernism we have chosen the Andalusian poet Manuel Machado (1874 - 1947), the older brother of Antonio. Machado in his poetry developed an exoticism (or escapism) with three facets: the elegant Bohemianism associated with Paris, the Moorish aspects and the popular poetry (the *cante hondo*) of Andalusia, and certain aspects of Spanish history. He earned a literary reputation with *Alma* (Soul) in 1902; surprisingly, in his aestheticism "soul" meant the glittering surface of things, not their inner spirit. Within his adopted aesthetic position, Machado created a poetry of consistently high quality and attractive theme, but rather early he began to lose his poetic inspiration, for his books after *Soul* became increasingly thin and lacking in substance. Ultimately Manuel Machado has come to represent the most perishable aspects of Darío's modernism — the preoccupation with form and a disengagement with real life.

Thus the Spanish poets of the twentieth century began and have continued to create their poetry under the influence of the various currents we have been sketching. In general, from Unamuno onward, the poets have followed the philosophical ideas of

Schopenhauer, Nietzsche, Bergson, Freud, and others, and the poetic currents associated with Poe, Baudelaire, Verlaine, and Mallarmé. At the same time most of them have keenly felt the loss of their solid Catholic tradition. The general influence of Krausism has seemed to further the Christian ethical ideals in a humanistic rather than a Christian setting. The two specific Spanish currents as represented by Unamuno's Castilian theme of the Generation of '98 and Darío's modernism, characterized by aesthetic concerns, have continued to compete against each other. While Unamuno and Machado pursued the Castilian theme (though not consistently), Jiménez elevated the aesthetic theme into his philosophy of poetry and existence. The Generation of '27 was at first closer to Jiménez, but in later years many of its members made a partial return to the concerns of Unamuno and Machado. The poets since the Civil War of 1936 - 39 have emphasized man in his social reality. As Jiménez emphasized, the overall unity of this modern period resides in the fact that the individual poet must assume the responsibility for carving out his own destiny from the multiple sources available to him in the past and the present.

CHAPTER 2

Miguel de Unamuno

H AVING departed from the chronological sequence of twentieth century Spanish poetry in our brief discussion of minor poets who followed Darío, we find it proper to begin our central chapters with the figure who is the "guide and master," not only of his own generation but also of later ones, Miguel de Unamuno y Jugo. In the much-repeated phrase of Count Keyserling, Unamuno was the greatest Spaniard — not just the greatest Spanish writer — since the painter Goya (who died in 1826). In the mold of the "great man" of Carlyle and Emerson, he exerted an influence upon many areas of national life. He was above all a figure of dynamic contradictions whose chief weapon was paradox. The essential term of his philosophy was to *agonize*, in its etymological sense of "to struggle." Fiercely traditional ("medieval," he called himself) in many ways, he was equally modern and revolutionary in his insistence upon the total freedom of conscience later demanded by the existentialists. Unamuno lived in the perpetual agitation of a love-hate, peace-war both for and against himself, Spain, Europe, even God himself.

Unamuno's formation was influenced essentially by the culture of two regions: the Basque country and Castile.[1] Born in Bilbao in 1864, he inherited from his Basque forbears a stubborn individualism which sometimes masked a feeling of inferiority. He was raised a normal Catholic in a traditional family, except that his father died when Miguel was still young. In 1880 Unamuno went down to Madrid for his college study, where he developed a disdain for the superficiality of the metropolitan atmosphere. Returning to Bilbao, he quietly married his childhood sweetheart Concha, and the couple began their family of eight children. In 1891, in one of the dreaded "oppositions," he won the chair of Greek at the University of Salamanca, where he spent his adult life. Here in old Castile he rapidly enlarged his vision to focus upon Castile and all of Spain. In 1924, partly because of his own intransigence, he was exiled alone to the Canary Islands and later to France by the dictator Primo de Rivera. Upon the advent of the Republic in 1931 he returned to Salamanca in momentary triumph, a prophet in his own country. He continued to participate in the tribulations of the Republic and died under house arrest in 1936, in the early months of the Civil War.

The essential stimulus for Unamuno's immense literary production can be traced to the intense religious crisis which he suffered in 1897, a crisis which was years in building and which recurred at intervals until his death.[2] In the rest of Europe this "crisis of conscience" developed gradually during the Renaissance, the Reformation, and the Enlightenment; Unamuno was the first Spaniard who fully assimilated all these fascinating but disturbing currents. In his early years he was attracted to the positivism of Comte and Spencer and the psychology of Wundt and James. A voracious reader in many languages, in maturity he studied the major sources of Western culture, especially the philosophy of Kant, Schopenhauer, Hegel, Rousseau, Kierkegaard, and Nietzsche, and the Christian tradition of the Bible, the mystics, and the German Protestant theologians. He began and continued as an essayist and a budding philosopher, but since he considered himself too passionate to bow to the discipline of philosophy, he ultimately decided that he must be mostly a poet, a poet of philosophical depth. Therefore, even his major philosophical works in prose, such as his well-known *The Tragic Sense of Life*, are written "poetically," that is, personally and passionately, without much regard for formal structure.

Unamuno began his poetic career around the age of thirty-five, when his ideas were already mature, and throughout his poetic career he continued to produce books of poetry that generally went against the prevailing mode, constantly changing his poetics and his habits of writing. In the heyday of *Modernismo* he declared that the poet should "think sentiment" and "feel thought," that form is superficial and substance is all that matters. After hesitating for nearly ten years, he finally published his first volume, severely entitled *Poesías (Poems)* in 1907. Then in five feverish months he produced his *Rosario de sonetos líricos* (Rosary of Lyric Sonnets) published in 1911. Around 1913 he began his *El Cristo de Velázquez (The Christ of Velázquez)*, now certain that blank verse in the manner of Milton was the only form of merit. Moreover, when he finally published the book in 1920, religious poetry was totally out of fashion. His *Teresa,* more or less in the Romantic manner, was written in a few months and published in 1923, when the various vanguard movements were beginning to flower. In *Teresa* he discovered the popular forms, such as the octosyllable. In *De Fuerteventura a París* (From Fuerteventura to Paris), published in 1925, he rediscovered the value of the traditional sonnet. Finally, in his last book, *Cancionero, diario íntimo* (Songbook, an Intimate Diary), begun in 1928 but published posthumously, he emphasized the forms of popular poetry and song, with Spanish assonance. Unamuno truly believed with Emerson that a "foolish consistency" should not restrict a great mind.

Unamuno's three principal themes concern the intimate discovery and regeneration of Spain without losing her character, his domestic preoccupations, and his quest for personal immortality — in short, Spain, family, and God.[3] Characteristic of him is his profound humanity; he preached himself as a man of flesh and blood. His poems therefore usually spring from a specific human situation in time and place. Although he seems (and is) fiercely self-centered, he is constantly reaching out to contact and even engulf the people and things of the world. This intimate pantheism with the things around him gives rise to a salient characteristic of his poetry, which the critic Concha Zardoya has perceptively called "humanation."[4] In his poetry Unamuno consistently humanizes the elements of nature and even God himself far beyond what is typical in poetry. For him the infinite expansion of consciousness was the aim of his life, and this reaching out to embrace and appropriate the universe a constant challenge. The tragedy of his existence was perhaps that he could never surrender himself to the response of the universe. In fact, he could never quite believe even in the reality of things outside himself; therefore in his philosophy life is an "agony" of infinite outreaching.

I *The Theme of Spain*

We shall begin with Unamuno's development of the Spanish or Castilian theme of the Generation of '98, for when he launched his poetic career, this was perhaps his most vital concern. Unamuno himself established the bases for the discussion of Spain's regeneration in his essay *En torno al casticismo* (Concerning the Essential Spanish Character), in which he emphasized the importance of the *paisaje* ("the land"), the effects of late-blooming mysticism in Spain, and the problems traceable to the excessive individualism of the Spanish type. Rather early realizing that his intimate Basque theme was excessively provincial, in Salamanca he responded to the high and austere Castilian tableland as being like himself. In his own person he felt at the same time the God-hunger of Spain's mystics, the bellicose impulses of Castile's warriors, and the fierce individualism of the Castilian peasant. In fact, Unamuno considered himself the typical Spaniard in conflict with himself.

Early in his career, he composed the poem specifically entitled "Castile," which has justly become an anthology piece.

> Tú me levantas, tierra de Castilla,
> en la rugosa palma de tu mano,
> al cielo que te enciende y te refresca,
> al cielo tu amo.

> You raise me up on high, Castilian land,
> In the rugged hollow of your hand,
> To the sky that kindles and refreshes you,
> To the sky, your master.

In the continuing stanzas, this land is "sinewy, austere, bathed in cloudless light"; land of "fierce hearts and mighty arms" in Spain's past; land which is all "summits." And in the concluding stanza, this land is an "altar," worthy of his most elevated songs.

> ¡Ara gigante, tierra castellana,
> a ese tu aire soltaré mis cantos,
> si te son dignos bajarán al mundo
> desde lo alto!

> Gigantic altar, Castilian land,
> I'll cast my songs in freedom upon your sky,
> Should they be worthy they'll descend toward earth
> From up on high!

This poem illustrates the essential characteristics of Unamuno's poetry. In the initial stanza, the simple but intimate and tactile metaphor of the Castilian plateau as a "rugged palm" is an example of the "humanizing" of the world in his poetry. Moreover, this vision is typically cast in a religious vein; his better songs are often "hymns," albeit hymns of paradoxical theme. Even in form "Castile" reveals Unamuno's subtle attempts at originality. Despite his attacks upon poets preoccupied with form, here in a typical stanza of hendecasyllables, he concludes with a pentasyllable, a favorite with him, which he modified after a classical Greek line. In his poems, this concluding pentasyllable serves to interrupt the rhythm of the stanza and forces us to dwell upon the sense of the concentrated line.

Perhaps Unamuno's favorite poem on the Castilian theme was his ode "Salamanca," devoted to the city rich in medieval and Renaissance tradition where he spent the adult years of his life. The ode is redolent with feeling for the historical efforts of the city, effects which produce a state of tranquility and permanence in the poet's heart. Salamanca is a "high grove of towers" touched by the mellow light of the "father Sun of Castile," a "forest of stones that history tore from the bowels of mother earth." He focuses particularly upon the "foliage of stone" that is the facade of the university, in Plateresque style where intricate figures are worked in the stone itself. Naturally, this timeless stone suggests permanence for the poet. Moreover, the poet evokes the figure of the great Renaissance humanist, Fray Luis de León, whose statue dominates a patio in the university. In his final invocation to Salamanca, Unamuno asks that his own presence also become a hallowed memory in this peaceful setting.

In later years, Unamuno continued to exploit the Castilian theme, with changing emphases. In political exile, he vented his wrath against the petty dictator and the squabbling politicians of Madrid in many of the sonnets of *From Fuerteventura to Paris*. On returning to Spain on the eve of the Republic, however, he recovered some of his equilibrium. Throughout his *Songbook*, he liked to play with brief lyrics concerning place names and the like, names of course meaningful to a Spaniard steeped in tradition and a philologist as well. A typical example is this one from the *Songbook* (no. 270):

> Ebro, Miño, Duero, Tajo,
> Guadiana y Guadalquivir,
>
> Rivers of Spain, what work
> Going down to the sea to die!

Obviously, in this play of names, Unamuno manages to infuse the archetypal symbol of the river as man's temporality.

II *The Domestic Theme*

As a man of "flesh and blood," Unamuno was grounded in living, with roots in a specific place — the Basque mountains, wide Castile, Salamanca, and, finally, his home and family. For Unamuno, his mother, his wife, and his children were "custom," or security, a security he paradoxically depended upon so that he could pursue his own troublesome liberty of thought. For Unamuno, his love for his wife Concha was never delight, surprise, or mystery; in fact, she became his "custom" — a deadly insult to the modern woman, but we assume his highest compliment to that lady herself. In one of the much-anthologized sonnets of the *Rosary of Lyric Sonnets* (CXIV), he utilizes one of Shakespeare's beautiful lines, "When to the sessions of sweet silent thought," to create an intimate scene of domestic bliss. In the background he hears the laughter of his children; the wife is sewing; he is reading Herodotus. The scene evokes in him an effective metaphor of tranquillity:

> Al tranquilo compás de un quieto aliento,
> ara en mí, como un manso buey la tierra,
> el dulce silencioso pensamiento.

> In tranquil rhythm of quiet encouragement,
> As patient oxen trod the earth, there plows
> In me a furrow of sweet silent thought.

In exile, Unamuno was uprooted from his family, and, with Spain in turmoil, his only peaceful news came from his home. The arrival of a picture of his wife stimulated him to write a double sonnet for his book *From Fuerteventura to Paris* (XXVI and XXVII), in which he reiterates her importance as his "custom." For Unamuno, custom is synonymous with "intra-history," the silent essence of life which endures. On Fuerteventura, apart from his companion, Unamuno actually enjoyed some brief moments of mystic union with the "feminine" sea as "wife" (in Spanish *mar* — "sea" — can be of either gender). Unamuno's intimations of immortality are usually centered in the feminine principle; for his awesome masculine God, in fact much like himself, seems doomed to uncertainty, struggle, and isolation.

Perhaps Unamuno's weirdest treatment of the domestic theme is his book *Teresa*, written in feverish haste in 1923, at a time when he was fearing the loss of his virility and creative powers. This collection of lyrics is the "novel" of Teresa and Rafael, Unamuno's prototype of the Spanish couple. In the book both are already dead; the poems were supposedly written by Rafael as Teresa was dying and passed on to Unamuno upon Rafael's death. Teresa is a symbol of domestic love, as Unamuno understood it; for him, all feminine

love was maternal, that is, compassion and suffering for the loved
one. That Teresa is young and virgin does not negate this, for
Unamuno wrote often of the "virgin mother" in Spain, one who
came to motherhood in such innocence that she never became aware
of her sexuality. As for her being young, for Unamuno, only the
young woman could feel the infinite suffering for her lover sufficiently strong to work his very salvation. Teresa in her simplicity
and purity teaches Rafael to suffer with God himself, and thus reach
salvation through love. When Unamuno glimpsed salvation, it was
through the feminine. For the cynical critic, then, *Teresa* may well
seem a satire upon the love-death orgies of the weaker Romantics,
but it is modern in that it is saturated with that "sickness unto
death" Unamuno discovered in Kierkegaard.

III   *The Quest for Immortality*

As we have demonstrated, Don Miguel de Unamuno believed in
the physical reality surrounding him (his Bilbao, his Salamanca, the
Gredos mountains), his home and family, and he devoted a part of
his lyric energies to them. But by far his central theme concerns his
hunger and thirst for the immortality of his individual soul, his entire being. With his religious orientation, this confirmation demanded the presence of a God both immanent and existent; that is,
the Christian God. And herein lay Unamuno's problem, his
rebellion, and his tragedy. While he sought desperately to become
the final prophet of Spanish Catholic tradition, he could not, and he
would not, submerge his unyielding individuality. Clearly, he is in
the tradition of Milton's Satan, Byron's Cain, Senancour's Ober-
mann, and Nietzsche's Superman. When we consider that he also
felt the influence of such contrasting Spanish figures as Loyola, St.
John of the Cross, and St. Theresa, we can understand the grounds
for his conflicts and paradoxes. While this conflict is at the heart of
all his poetry (and work), it is in the *Rosary of Lyric Sonnets* that he
gives it the most concentrated expression.

In an early sonnet in the *Rosary* (XI), Unamuno tantalizes us with
the title "Our Secret," followed by these fine lines:

> No me preguntes más, es mi secreto,
> secreto para mí terrible y santo. . . .

> Ask me no more, for this my secret is,
> A secret terrible and holy in my heart. . . .

The beginning phrase paraphrases Tennyson's melancholy line,
"Ask me no more, for fear I should reply," but Unamuno goes
further, declaring that in the "obscure abyss" of his soul there is a
"fatidic turn" which must not be trespassed. And he concludes with
a twisted paraphrase of Socrates: "Mortal, know thyself, but not in
everything." If man knows himself completely, the knowledge is
overwhelming: the secret is terrible because it involves probable annihilation of the soul; it is "holy" because only this secret spurs man
to superhuman, to godly efforts to save himself.

Unamuno inherited in fullness the two currents in the Western
tradition, rationalism and the Christian faith, or the head and the
heart. Doggedly, he set out to utilize both for his salvation, and, in a
positive moment, he foresaw a certain kind of victory. In "Reason
and Faith" (LIII), he synthesized the program of his mature years.

> Levanta de la fe el blanco estandarte
> sobre el polvo que cubre la batalla. . .

> Raise high aloft faith's streaming pennant white
> Above the dust that covers the battlefield. . .

But Unamuno's faith is not the peace (the resignation) that follows
battle; his God "abominates him who surrenders." In bloody
struggle, man must make his way, with or without reason, with or
without faith. In fact, as the scholar Julián Marías has insisted,
Unamuno rather hastily abandoned rationalism as a tool. But he
endeavored to replace it with the all-embracing idea of indomitable
human will of both head and heart as the efficacious philosophy, in
the tradition of Nietzsche. In a moving sonnet to Nietzsche, perhaps
significantly numbered (C), Unamuno records that Nietzsche cursed
Christ, "the archetypical superman," because he could not be
Christ. Because of this great effort, Unamuno concludes ironically
that Nietzsche died "free from reason," that is, insane. Unamuno
fails to add that he must have envisioned himself as a Nietzsche
whom the struggle would not render insane; he imagined himself a
new Don Quixote, sane in his divine madness.

This subtlety of thought is metaphysically expressed in the much-
quoted paradoxical sonnet "The Prayer of the Atheist" (XXXIX):

> Oye mi ruego Tú, Dios que no existes,
> y en tu nada recoge estas mis quejas. . . .

> Hear Thou my cry, God who does not exist,
> And in thy nothingness reap my complaints. . . .

How can the religiously oriented poet be an atheist who prays?
When the atheist feels that God does not exist, he doesn't, says
Unamuno, because for him God is essentially *immanent*. He con-
cludes, playing with this same problem:

> Sufro yo a tu costa,
> Dios no existente, pues si Tú existieras
> existiría yo también de veras.

> I suffer at your expense,
> God nonexistent, for if Thou didst exist
> Then I would verily exist also.

Unamuno as a philologist never tired of subtilizing with the verbs
ex-istir and *in-sistir*. Obviously, *existir* means "to be *outside*," outside the poet himself. He could believe in the nature of God as *Being*, but he could never believe in God's *existence* outside his own
heart.

Unamuno carries this theme to its ultimate conclusion in one of
his most powerful sonnets in the *Rosary* (CXXI). Called ironically
"The Union with God," it begins with the initial line quoted
directly from Michaelangelo:

> *Querría, Dios, querer lo que no quiero;*
> fundirme en Ti, perdiendo mi persona,
> este terrible yo por el que muero. . . .

> *I'd like to want, my Lord, what I want not;*
> To melt my heart in Thine, my person losing,
> This dreadful "I" for which I live near death. . . .

The stanzas of the sestet expand this idea of willful rebellion.
Although the poet keeps repeating "Thy will be done, Father!" his
will refuses to submit:

> Pero dentro de mí resuena el grito
> del eterno Luzbel, del que quería
> ser, ser de veras, ¡fiero desacato!

> But within the heart of me resounds the cry
> Of that eternal Lucifer, of him who yearned
> To be, to be in truth, fierce profanation!

Predictably, the church in Spain rose up in arms against this blatant
heresy, often couched in twisted biblical passages, but Unamuno,
always "against this and that," sardonically welcomed his chastise-
ment, saying that it was proper for the church to "scratch away its
fleas" (XLVII).

In the foregoing discussion we have concentrated upon the
sonnets of Unamuno, because in a restricting form he was forced to
curb a tendency to prolixity. Among his longer lyric poems,
however, "Aldebarán," written in his variant of the traditional *silva*,
has become justly famous. Aldebarán, the star which is the eye of
the bull in the constellation Taurus, was chosen specifically because
it is already ancient as indicated by its reddish color. The poem is a
long meditative monologue, in which Unamuno the great in-
terrogator indicates his modern awareness of time in relation to the
universe itself. As late as Keats, after 1800, at least the stars were
"steadfast," or eternal, but Unamuno knew that the modern
astronomer has stripped away man's last metaphor of eternity: not
only are the stars in stunning isolation, but also all of them are
doomed to die, like man. Unamuno's poem reflects this knowledge,
and inevitably he reaches the death of Aldebarán itself:

> ¿A dónde Dios, por su salud luchando,
> te habrá de segregar, estrella muerta,
> Aldebarán?
> ¿A qué tremendo muladar de mundos?

> And where is God, for his own health struggling,
> Going to find a place for you, dead star,
> Aldebarán?
> In what tremendous dunghill of worlds?

This rough metaphor of the dunghill conveys Unamuno's dismay,
for science has provided us no image more horrifying than that of
the dead star, infinitely compressed, infinitely dark, and thus utterly
lost to man's probing telescopes.

Unamuno's grand attempt to synthesize his major metaphysical
preoccupations and themes is concentrated in his book-length poem
The Christ of Velázquez.[5] Despite his near-mania to assert the
uniqueness of his own being, Unamuno desired paradoxically to be
the prophet and voice of the Spanish people. With certain intuition he
seized upon the image of Don Diego Velázquez's painting of Christ
upon the Cross, found in the Prado Museum, in order to "formulate

the faith of his people." It is a study in stark black and white, with Christ's white body standing out in the center and with his dark hair hanging over his face. Unamuno's poem is an extended lyric meditation upon this figure and what his sacrifice means. In the traditional parts of the poem, Unamuno utilizes salient passages from the Bible and reworks the symbols for Christ in the manner of Fray Luis de León's *Los nombres de Cristo*. But in essence *The Christ of Velázquez* reveals Unamuno's unorthodox ideas and personal emphases concerning Christ. For the 2,538 lines of the poem Christ remains upon the Cross: this is Unamuno's way of emphasizing life and love as suffering, and of obscuring the Resurrection. For Unamuno, Christ is indeed a divine figure, but he is "all man," and his divinity is an *achievement*, not the divine plan of God. In fact, Unamuno's unconventional theology is clearly revealed in one of his flat hendecasyllables: "Tú hiciste a Dios, Señor, para nosotros" ("Christ, you made God for all the rest of us"; I, vii). In short, whereas Milton set out to justify the ways of God to man, Unamuno is attempting to justify the ways of man to God.

In his hunger for immortality of any and all kinds, Miguel de Unamuno succeeded in becoming perhaps the outstanding cultural figure in twentieth-century Spain. Although he began in the middle of his life, naturally he set out to make himself the greatest lyric poet. In this he failed, but his reputation as one of the major poets has grown steadily with the passing years. As Jiménez emphasized, modern Spanish poetry is born with Darío, who represents aesthetic freedom, and with Unamuno, who represents freedom of conscience. As we have stressed, Unamuno was the first major figure in Spain to free himself from Catholic dogma, but this freedom burdened him with the problem of creating his own metaphysics, torn between Catholicism and modern philosophical ideas. This essential conflict provides the tension of his poetry and gives it high seriousness. As a poet, Unamuno must be selected severely. As an overreaction against Darío's preoccupation with form, initially he was prone to write discursive poems of chillingly common expression; however, in his reaction he gradually found a way to his own originality. For example, whereas the *modernistas* were fond of musical, complete lines which "lulled" the reader, in his sonnets Unamuno deliberately utilized a harsh enjambment which awakens and even annoys us but forces us to concentrate upon the theme. While the *modernistas* cultivated a vocabulary that was "beautiful" or exotic, Unamuno brandished the homely and roughly intimate words of the Castilian tradition. Surely his sonnets are his best poems, although every one of them is marked (like life, he would have said) with a flaw or two. Since Unamuno preached "thinking sentiment and feeling thought," early critics argued that his poems are loaded with *ideas*. This is simply incorrect, for as serious readers we *feel* with him, against him, or both at the same time. And we are disquieted, goaded to a greater self-realization by the example of his embattled spirit. Although the purist will protest, Unamuno the poet is inseparable from Unamuno the man of flesh and blood and bone.

CHAPTER 3

Antonio Machado

A NTONIO MACHADO gradually became known as the poet of
the Generation of '98, even though he joined it late, mainly
because Unamuno was appreciated basically as a prose writer,
Azorín and Baroja surprisingly wrote no poetry, and Jiménez was
considered outside the Generation. Machado was that rarest of
beings, a man and even a great literary figure who never made a
declared enemy — even a competitor like Jiménez retained an admiration for him. While still a relatively young man, he became
something of a "good gray poet" for everyone, a stereotype which
even a late renaissance of his vital energies could not dispel. As a
mature thinker he harbored revolutionary ideas against both church
and state and finally began to disseminate them, but because of his
gentle manner much of the wrath of these establishments fell instead upon the belligerent Unamuno. Even in his autumn love for
"Guiomar," a lady married and with children, his personal and
poetic conduct was such that his reputation emerged enhanced.
After he died in the tragic aftermath of the Civil War, his reputation
as a man and poet has become consecrated.

Antonio Machado y Ruiz was born in Seville in 1875, in a spacious
home graced with patios, fountains, lemon trees, and the brilliant
flowers of Andalusia.[1] His family soon moved to Madrid, where he
attended the Free Institute for a time. As his family came upon hard
times, he spent his youth in a semi-Bohemian existence — innocent,
to be sure — in Madrid. Coming under Unamuno's influence,
Machado prepared himself for teaching French in the secondary
schools. In 1907 he went up to the highlands of Soria to begin his
career, and there he met and married a young lass named Leonor.
When she died tragically of tuberculosis in 1912, he fled to Baeza
and remained there for seven years. From 1919 to 1931 he taught in
Segovia, but he spent much time in Madrid, where he and his

35

brother Manuel composed some successful plays. Around 1926 he met Guiomar, his poetic name for his autumn love, and this affair endured until the Civil War. He wrote his important prose work *Juan de Mairena* during this later period. During the war he served the Republican cause in Madrid and Valencia and died in exile in France in 1939.

As a poet, Antonio Machado's production is very limited, for his *Poesías completas* (Complete Poems) include only four books, one of these of secondary importance. Since Machado always suffered difficulties in organizing his books, we shall discuss his poetry under three fairly well defined periods.[2] The first, "The Poet and the Inner World," embraces the second edition of his first major book, *Soledades, Galerías y otros poemas* (Solitudes, Galleries and Other Poems; 1907). The second period, "The Poet Looks Outward," includes his essential book *Campos de Castilla* (Fields of Castile; 1912) and a bit of *Nuevas canciones* (New Songs). The third, "The Poet as Metaphysician," includes his "Proverbs and Songs" and his *Cancionero apócrifo,* parts of which express in prose his "poet's metaphysics." Since his distinct poetic voice remained somewhat the same throughout his career, there is an underlying unity in all his poetry, despite a pronounced diversity of theme and manner. Certainly the growing body of criticism of his individual books indicates that Machado created outstanding poetry in all three periods.

I *The Poet and the Inner World*

Stimulated by the influences of Bécquer, Darío, and the French poet Paul Verlaine, Antonio Machado accepted his calling as a poet and published the first edition of *Solitudes* in 1903, the expanded edition *Solitudes, Galleries and Other Poems* following in 1907. In his title *Solitudes,* Machado appropriated a term rich in historical connotations, but he enriches it with the modern sense of existential isolation and loneliness. As he expressed it later, Machado retains the sense of subjectivity inherent in the term "solitude": "The dominant ideology was essentially subjective; art was disintegrating, and the poet . . . pretended to sing only to himself."[3] For Machado this solitude provided an opportunity for a deepening of the spirit, as he analyzed it in his prologue to the second edition of *Solitudes:* "I thought that the poetic element was not the word for its sound values, nor color, nor line, nor a complex of sensations, but a deep palpitation of the spirit."[4] This "deep palpitation of the spirit" became his trademark throughout his poetic career.

While he realized later that his *Solitudes* was not a "systematic realization" of his aesthetic purposes, in it Antonio Machado projected himself firmly as a *poeta en el tiempo,* a "poet in time." In *Solitudes* he is a poet of temporality essentially through intuition of time, as is normal in poetry; gradually Machado the metaphysician began to analyze the fruits of his intuition with great clarity. In a defining poem of a single stanza (XXXV)[5] he fixes his situation:

> Al borde del sendero un día nos sentamos.
> Ya nuestra vida es tiempo, y nuestra sola cuita
> son las desesperantes posturas que tomamos
> para aguardar . . . Mas Ella no faltará a la cita.

> One evening by the wayside we sat down.
> Our life is now time, our sole concern
> The desperate postures we assume to await . . .
> But She that final hour will not spurn.

Of course the Lady is Death herself, but the key phrase is the assertion "Our life is now time." Machado's intense preoccupation with time is ultimately traceable to his "crisis of conscience," his loss of the Catholic faith. This loss was critical and profound, and much of the tension in his poetry can be traced to the resulting importance attached to temporal existence. He develops this temporal theme through a limited number of traditional symbols, such as the fountain, the road, and the river.

Machado is also the *poeta en sueños,* the "poet of memory." For Machado as for Bécquer to be *en sueños* is a mental state achieved in the most intense wakeful hours; naturally it involves a flight from humdrum reality. In this state of reverie the poet looks into his soul and attempts to expand the power of memory, the remembrance of things past, in the manner of Proust, whose writings afford the model of the time-memory theme. Quite a number of poems in *Solitudes* emphasize the theme of the power of memory with subtle suggestiveness, such as this lyric which represents a pure moment in the poet's existence:

> Tarde tranquila, casi
> con placidez de alma,
> para ser joven, para haberlo sido
> cuando Dios quiso, para
> tener algunas alegrías . . . lejos
> y poder dulcemente recordarlas.

Tranquil afternoon, almost
With placidity of soul . . .
To be, to have been young
When God was on our side;
To know some joys . . . then distance,
And sweetly to remember.

While impressionistic poets (such as the early Jiménez) found aesthetic joy in the present moment, it seems that Machado is eager to rush by the experience itself for the greater pleasure of reelaborating it in his memory.

As a poet of memory explored, intensified, and at times almost created, Machado discovered a special richness in the recollections of childhood. From his living past he gradually settled upon a permanent image, that of the patio of his first home in Seville, with its fountain and citrus trees and brilliant flowers. In general, childhood is evoked as a time of plenitude, of promise, and of innocence. He remembers especially the voices of the children chanting against the silence of the dark old plazas. His symbol for the plenitude of childhood is the rounded fruits of the citrus trees, the orange and the lemon.

In one of his typical poems of childhood memory the poet returns to the patio of his early years to focus upon the "golden fruits," but in this poem the fountain, his symbol of time, begins to replace the fruits.

El limonero lánguido suspende
una pálida rama polvorienta
sobre el encanto de la fuente limpia,
y allá en el fondo sueñan
los frutos de oro . . .

The lemon tree languidly suspends
A pale, dust-laden branch
Above the enchantment of the limpid fountain,
And in the shimmering depths
The golden fruits are dreaming.

When he was a child, with his mother's help he could actually reach these golden fruits with his hand; now they have become "dream," a pale image at the bottom of the fountain.

Another important aspect of his theme of time and memory are the poems in which he searches for love and lost youth. The reticent poet is desperately seeking to create "fiestas of love," but it is always distant: "Among the golden poplars, / Far off, the shadow of love awaits" (LXXX). In one of his much discussed lyrics (LXII) he succeeds in reverie in capturing a tremulous vision of love which seems real:

> ¡El limonero florido,
> el cipresal del huerto,
> el prado verde, el sol, el agua, el iris . . .
> el agua en tus cabellos!
>
> The lemon trees in bloom,
> The garden's cypress grove,
> Green meadow, sun, water, the rainbow's arch . . .
> The raindrops in your hair!

But a sudden disturbance shatters his reverie, and as he returns to reality his "dream" vanishes like "soap bubbles in the wind."

The occasional tone of lyric exuberance is overshadowed in Machado by a somber note, exemplified in another poem, justly become an anthology piece, in which he develops the theme of lost passion (XI). Here the poet introduces two of his major symbols, the road and the "clear afternoon." Upon the road he is a wayfarer forever seeking love, life, and ultimately God in time that is vanishing. His time is the clear afternoon, when it is already late, but a time when the harsh truths of existence are seen with utmost clarity. The poem begins with one of the essential Machadian lines, "I go along dreaming roads/ In the afternoon," and he goes on to describe the memory of a passion which he thought was unbearable:

> Yo voy cantando, viajero
> a lo largo del sendero . . .
> — La tarde cayendo está —
> "En el corazón tenía
> la espina de una pasión;
> logré arrancármela un día:
> ya no siento el corazón.
>
> I make my way in song, wayfarer
> Upon an endless way . . .
> — Evening is overtaking day —
> "Within my heart I had a thorn
> Of passion true and real;
> One day I snatched it out in scorn:
> My heart now nothing feels.

In freeing himself of the thorn, however, he destroys his passion also, and finally begs for the return of the thorn with its necessary pain. In his poetry of love the poet's experience has been so thin that even his power of memory will not save it, and he abandons the theme in despair.

Forsaking childhood, youth, and love, Machado turns to his metaphysical preoccupations in one of the longest and most essential poems of *Solitudes* (XIII), in which he develops the ancient water symbols of river and sea. From the beginning he was drawn to Manrique's famous elegy on the death of his father, with its well-known lines "Our lives are rivers flowing down/ Unto the sea, which sea is death." As is typical the poet is upon the road, perhaps specifically upon the Roman bridge which spans the Duero River, at first lulled by the twilight landscape. But his sense of temporality overwhelms him as the very waters seem to speak and tell him that all is "nothingness."

In his searching and questioning toward the end of *Solitudes*, the poet plunges deeper into the "galleries of remembrance" which are his consciousness and discovers that a "divine truth,/ Trembling with fear" is waiting to burst forth. Gone are his earlier aesthetic preoccupations; now his reverie becomes attached to an "eternal labor," and he will "dream" to an ethical purpose. The poem which most adequately expresses Machado's triumphs and failures at this point is "Last Night as I Lay Sleeping" (LXIX). Like a lullaby, this lyric is clearly in the mystic tradition. In the basic stanzas the poet dreams that there are a fountain flowing, a beehive working, and a sun shining inside his breast. Finally he dreams it is God himself:

> Anoche cuando dormía
> soñé — ¡bendita ilusión! —
> que era Dios que tenía
> dentro de mi corazón.

> Last night as I lay sleeping
> I dreamed — Oh illusion blest! —
> That it was God I had
> Deep down inside my breast.

The soothing rhythms of the poem should not deceive us as to the sense of the stanza. In the Christian mystics such as St. Theresa and St. John of the Cross, in the stage of union the soul comes to *know* God directly; here, not only is the poet dreaming that he has found

God, but even the dream is an illusion, however blessed the moment.

Machado's mood of anguish deepens in the poems that follow. His once "clear afternoon" is beclouded like his soul: "It is an ashgray, gloomy afternoon,/ Bedraggled like my poor soul" (LXXVII). In his anguish he is stumbling along like a drunk, "Forever seeking God among the mists." From this point, his very inspiration is threatened, for the human pain which provided the substance for his poetic labor is now overwhelming him. His poetic venture in *Solitudes* ends in a confession of defeat; the poet of yesterday becomes the philosopher of today, a philosopher perishing in his tragic thought.

Antonio Machado's *Solitudes, Galleries and Other Poems* has attained an important position as an example of the renovation in modern Spanish poetry. At the end of his long career his fellow poet Jiménez declared in an undisputed statement: "It fell to Machado and to me to initiate in our modern poetry the expression of the inner spirit [*lo interior*]."[6] Machado himself pointed out that *Solitudes* was the first book of modern Spanish poetry from which the anecdotal was proscribed. Although many of the lyrics seem to begin in the impressionistic manner, by technique Machado is a symbolist poet, working and reworking a few essential symbols. Already some of the poems and particular lines have become a permanent addition to the Spanish literary heritage.

II   *The Poet Looks Outward:* Fields of Castile

When Antonio Machado went up to Soria in 1907 he was ready to turn away from the self-enforced isolation of *Solitudes* and begin to look outward. Settled in Soria, he experienced directly the influence of the Castilian landscape and began to study seriously the writings of his contemporaries who were to be called the Generation of '98, especially Unamuno. Machado adopted Unamuno's central ideas and began to explore these "Castilian" themes in his poetry. With the publication of *Fields of Castile* in 1912, Machado earned late membership in the Generation of '98. His approach in this book of looking outward toward the reality of Spain, the Spanish landscape, and his personal life situation endured for several years, until around 1924. There are perhaps three major themes in the poetry of this period. The most important of course deals with the problem and destiny of Spain, often called the Castilian theme, which includes the Soria poems. The second concerns a group of *elogios*, or poems of praise for worthy colleagues also striving to regenerate Spain and Spanish literature. The third theme consecrates the memory of the poet's love for Leonor in Soria, a love simple but real, the loss of which threatened to turn Machado away from the real world.

After an initial "Portrait" of the poet himself, *Fields of Castile* commences with a section of poems which explore various facets of the Castilian theme, landscape, and character, ending with a series specifically on the landscape around Soria. In all subsequent editions he continued to place "A orillas del Duero" ("On the Banks of the Duero"; XCVIII) in a commanding position; indeed this poem has proved to be Machado's outstanding statement of the Castilian theme in the "bitter" manner. In the poem, Romantic in the manner of Wordsworth, the poet on a July day leaves the town on his walk, struggles up the foothills surrounding Soria, and observes the landscape realistically; then he begins to meditate upon Castile in a larger context. In the weighty Alexandrine couplets of the poem, his theme emerges in the form of a refrain:

> Castilla miserable, ayer dominadora,
> Envuelta en sus andrajos desprecia cuanto ignora.
>
> Wretched Castile, triumphant yesterday,
> Wrapped in her rags, she scorns all change today.

Then the panorama before him is described in martial imagery. A rounded hill is a "decorated shield"; the reddish heights are "scattered remnants of an ancient suit of armor"; the Duero curves around Soria "like a crossbow's arc" — one of Machado's persistent metaphors. This imagery of war suggests a favorite theme of the Generation of '98, that of Castile as "warlike and mystic." The poet goes on to lament the disappearance of the great "captains" such as Cortez and Balboa, and the fact that the great religious figures such as Loyola and St. John of the Cross have been replaced by impassive and nameless figures in the monasteries. Finally his bitter meditation ends, and the poet climbs down from the mountain as night is falling.

In a series of lyrics entitled "Campos de Soria" ("Fields of Soria") Machado actually "created" Soria for himself and the rest of Spain. This "pure Soria" (the words upon the town's crest), with its silver-tinted hills, gray heights, and rocks of reddish hue, sank deeply into Machado's consciousness; for him Soria represented the timelessness of Spain, since it was a stronghold in Roman times and a bastion against the Moors in the Middle Ages. For him, the landscape existed in such reality that even the rocks "dreamed." And when he left Soria, it passed into his "dream" as a set of permanent images. The bright poplars along the banks of the Duero, which curves in its "crossbow's arc" around Soria, became symbols for his belonging to the land, a unity he was never to feel again.

During this Castilian period of looking outward, Machado, always a generous spirit, conceived the idea of honoring those "select spirits" who were also working toward a new Spain in a series of *elogios*. In these poems of praise, Machado attempted initially to adopt the point of view of the figure chosen, and then to continue in a channel acceptable to the ideals of both himself and the subject. These "select spirits" of course include Unamuno and his brother poets Darío and Jiménez; Azorín, who also exploited the Castilian theme with enduring success; Ortega y Gasset, whom Machado admired even though his philosophy of Europeanizing Spain clashed with Machado's; and Francisco de Giner, the renowned educator and founder of the Free Institute. Although this type of poem is generally out of fashion, Machado's *elogios* have been repeatedly quoted as expressing the essence of the figure praised.

In his third important theme of the period of *Fields of Castile*, Machado expresses the personal experience of his love for Leonor in Soria, principally *in morte*. Of the beginnings, growth, and fullness of this love there is no record; his first poem concerning her is "A un olmo seco" ("To a Withered Elm"; CXV), in which he observes that in a miracle of spring the old elm has put out a few leaves. He pleads for "another miracle of spring" so that Leonor, in failing health, might recover. But she dies soon afterward, and the poet is cast adrift. In Baeza the next spring, however, he recovers his equilibrium and writes one of his most remembered poems, "To José María Palacio" (CXXV). In the epistolary form of the Renaissance, he writes his friend Palacio in Soria in April, asking if spring has reached the high country, if his favorite aspects of nature — the white-flowered brambles, the cherry tree, the white daisies, and the storks which flutter awkwardly around the bell tower — have yet returned. Then, almost as an afterthought, he asks Palacio to take the first-blooming roses up to the Espina cemetery, "where her country is," and place them upon her grave. This simple but moving poem is saved from excessive sentimentality by his use of the epistolary form and his focus upon the rebirth of spring. In later years the memory of this human love remained as a soft glow of piety.

Despite a certain raggedness of structure typical of Machado, *Fields of Castile* is a solid human document more and more difficult for modern poets to write. It is his effort, successful for a time, to look outward toward the real world of Spanish cultural and political problems, the Castilian landscape, and the creation of a personal life. This venture ends in another "defeat" for the lyric poet, however, for Soria and his human love retreat into the "dream" and his world becomes ironically "metaphysical." Although this traditional book fell out of fashion in the generation of Guillén and Lorca, the socially oriented generations following the Civil War have accepted *Fields of Castile* as a minor classic.

III   *The Poet as Metaphysician*

The third and final period in Antonio Machado's poetic production is complex, difficult, and shot through with paradoxes, but it is ultimately rewarding as the culmination of his poetic career.[7] By 1925, Machado was experiencing a powerful desire for a personal rebirth while at the same time he was feeling the pressure of the new generation of poets forcing him toward a renovation of his poetry. Since he had always wavered between poetry and philosophy, it was natural that he attempt to blend them together, ultimately reaching this conclusion: "Some day poets and philosophers will exchange roles. The poets will sing of their astonishment in the presence of great metaphysical deeds; the philosopher will speak to us of anguish, the essentially poetic anguish of being close to nothingness."[8]

Machado's attempt to blend the philosophical and the poetic begins in a rather simple way in his "Proverbs and Songs," the first series of which appeared in *Fields of Castile*. But in the strange and difficult *Cancionero apócrifo* (Apocryphal Songbook), written between 1921 and 1933, Machado elaborates his metaphysical ideas both in prose and in a group of major poems which exemplify his metaphysics. Secure behind his *persona* of Abel Martín (note the initials), poet and philosopher, he dwells first upon his idea of "the essential heterogeneity of being," that each individual consciousness is encapsulated in its own being. But his consciousness suffers an infinite "nostalgia" toward the other. This Other is first woman, for he confesses ironically in a *copla* that "Without woman there is neither begetting nor knowledge." Because of the essential heterogeneity of being, the beloved is "metaphysically impossible" in reality, she exists only in "absence"; but she is therefore "poetically possible," for the poor poet can and must pursue his lonely but essential task of singing to and for her in his existential world.

From his rich but tormented love for Guiomar the aging poet creates "in the manner of Abel Martín" a brief collection of some of his most intense lyrics. In his bitter vein, his "Recollections of Dream, Fever, and Nightmare" (CLXXI), carefully orchestrated in twelve sections, is perhaps Machado's most impressive single poem, though certainly not his most typical. Whereas before the dream was a controlled state of reverie, in this poem the dream sequence is presented in the Freudian manner, with the usual embroilment of time and event, hope and guilt. In his nightmare the poet confuses his sanctified love for Leonor with his present love for Guiomar; he is first tormented by jealousy and then racked by guilt. His "road" becomes a maze of streets and blind alleys, so that finally he can only sing bitterly "Love always turns to ice."

With the passage of the years the poet retreats into time and memory, and his now hopeless yearning exudes from his tender "Songs for Guiomar" (CLXXII, CLXXIV). At the beginning he believed in her "dark, rose-tinted flesh" at the seashore; now in memory he retreats with her into a garden out of time:

> En un jardín te he soñado,
> alto, Guiomar, sobre el río,
> jardín de un tiempo cerrado
> con verjas de hierro frío.

> I've dreamed you in a garden high,
>   Guiomar, above the river;
> A garden with cold iron grilles,
>   Closed to time forever.

For once he dreams that a "goddess and her prince" are escaping beyond the limits of this earth, beyond the seas, even beyond the pursuit of God himself, but the ethical Machado could only imagine a love free, never live it. Finally he sadly declares that "All love is fantasy," that the beloved may never exist; yet the only meaningful event in life is the brief miracle of love, and the only enduring thing is the poetry which that miracle inspires.

While stressing the ultimate subjectivity of everything connected with his consciousness, Machado nevertheless felt a persistent urge to overcome that subjectivity by recognizing an incurable yearning toward *Otherness.* In his lyric poetry, this yearning becomes "erotic" and goes toward woman, the beloved. In the social sphere, it becomes fraternal love, exemplified clearly in Jesus. In the *Apocryphal Songbook* the ultimate yearning is of course toward God. For Machado, as for Unamuno, God is a being that "we all make," or help to make; that is, God is immanent in the human consciousness. His final defeat in his pursuit of God is projected in a massive and complex sonnet entitled "Al gran Cero" ("To the Great Zero"). In the sonnet, which begins as a travesty of the Creation scene in Genesis, God triumphantly creates the "empty, universal egg" of Nothingness. This Nothingness is the complement of the poet's consciousness, just as the beloved is the "impossible" complement of the poet as lover. Finally the sonnet suggests that the "Great Zero" is God himself. For Machado this is the tragic lesson that man learns on the road of life, that he is utterly alone in the universe, but he can and should sing his song at the edge of Nothingness.

Toward the end of the *Apocryphal Songbook* there are a number of impressive poems on death. In "Death of Abel Martín" (CLXXV), Machado reaches perhaps the highest peak of emotional intensity in all his work. For the reader who has patiently absorbed his poetry up to this moment, the opening lines evoke a chill of emotional identification with their images typical of the poet:

Los últimos vencejos revolean
en torno al campanario;
los niños gritan, saltan, se pelean.
En su rincón, Martín el solitario.
¡La tarde, casi noche, polvorienta,
la algazara infantil, y el vocerío,
a la par, de sus doce en sus cincuenta!

The last dark martins flutter in profusion
Around the cathedral tower;
The children shout, leap, scuffle in confusion.
And in his corner, Martín in loneliness.
Dust-laden afternoon, just as the dusk appears —
The childhood din, his roar of consciousness —
Their dozen blended with his fifty years!

In the "solitude" which follows, the alter ego whose death the poet is experiencing is alone with the substance of his memories. First there is his pursuit of love, which he now calls "sacred oblivion"; in fact the beloved becomes fused with Death herself. Even more important is his final "great knowledge of the Zero," of the God equated with Nothingness. In the last scene, ultimate human fatigue follows upon his anguish. Although he utters a cry for salvation, when he raises the "limpid glass" to his lips for the final draught, it is filled, not with life-giving water or saving light, but with shadow, "pure shadow." Truly this is one of the most moving poems on death in Spanish literature.

Antonio Machado was a poet of insistently tragic voice, in many ways comparable to our Robert Frost; yet he has come to represent the indomitability of the human spirit. As we have emphasized, three times he sallied forth on his poetic quest, and three times he fell back in various kinds of defeat. However, each time he accumulated something of his *word in time*, so that gradually he became the *poet in time, poeta en el tiempo*. While all the major Spanish poets of the twentieth century are also poets in time, Machado appropriated this phrase for himself and later poets have graciously conceded it to him. A poet traditional in form and intensely human in theme, for a time he seemed insufficiently modern for the generation of Lorca and Guillén, but gradually his reputation as a man and a poet has become consecrated in all of Spain and even in Hispanic America. Machado's poetry, like Unamuno's, retains a Spanish flavor, in contrast to that of Jiménez or Guillén, which is more universal. But in his person and in his poetry, as the young writers of today haltingly express it, Antonio Machado "awakens a tenderness difficult to explain." As long as our present mood of anguish and searching endures, Antonio Machado, grounded in his Spanish earth but cast adrift philosophically, will continue to provide an example of the nobility of the human spirit.

CHAPTER 4

Juan Ramón Jiménez

J UAN RAMÓN JIMÉNEZ is above all a poet's poet — a master, an inspiration, a challenge, a standard even for poets. In his makeup he exemplifies all the complexities and paradoxes expected of a great figure. With the arrogance of a titan he could ultimately make this sweeping pronouncement: "I well realize that in Spanish literature there is no other comparable example of a poetic work as complete, which stretches from the romantic of youthful age to the intellectual and metaphysical of maturity."[1] Following in the tradition of those astonishing Spanish creators such as Lope de Vega, Quevedo, and Galdós, Jiménez published more than forty volumes of poetry, a dozen of them perfectly unified in both theme and form, and yet he always swore he destroyed much more than he published. Indulged by his family for the first half of his life and by a devoted wife for the second, he lived and created in his splendid isolation, "the anguish of the adolescent, the young man, the mature man who feels himself unattached, alone, apart in his beautiful vocation."[2] That vocation was poetry, for him a great movement of enthusiasm and liberty toward beauty. Ultimately his pursuit of beauty is fused with his ethics: "I live in a spiritual asceticism, I live for poetry, for art, and not only in poetry but in everything I seek to adjust my life to a norm of moral perfection."[3] Since many of his later contemporaries felt that moral perfection should be achieved in struggling with humanity, Jiménez's reputation has continued to suffer ups and downs in comparison with those of more humanistic poets such as Machado and Unamuno.

Jiménez's life reveals the expected contradictions of a person of his extreme sensitivity.[4] He was born in 1881 in Palos de Moguer, for him a "white marvel" of a town on the Andalusian coast. Since his family was then relatively wealthy, he grew up in privileged circumstances. Very early he began to flood the local journals with

48

adolescent verses, and in 1900 he went to Madrid to seek poetic fame. When he returned to Moguer, the sudden death of his father precipitated a nervous breakdown, and he spent the next year in a sanatorium in France. In 1916 he traveled to New York to marry Zenobia Camprubí, who became wife, mother, companion, and his shield against the outside world. In 1936 Jiménez returned to America, first stopping in Cuba and then residing in various university locations in the United States. In 1951 the couple settled permanently in Puerto Rico, where Jiménez lectured in the growing university there. When his beloved Zenobia died in 1956, three days after he received the Nobel Prize, Jiménez fell into a depression from which he never recovered. He died in 1958.

For Jiménez, his life was unimportant; his *Obra*, his poetic works, representing fifty years of incessant creation, was everything. And this extensive poetry presents an awesome challenge to the critic. Although there are a half-dozen excellent books on his poetry, no one of them embraces it in totality. In what has become a stock (and yet exact) phrase, Jiménez is a poet of the ineffable, that which is inexpressible; for him poetry *is* the expression of the ineffable by means of symbols. Jiménez was a Platonist who believed that the "Ideas" of Beauty, God, Love actually exist; therefore the poet's task is to utilize a correspondence of symbols to "suggest" these ideas so intensely that they are created for the poet and reader.

In striving to give shape and substance to the ineffable, Jiménez gradually utilized most of the accumulated techniques of previous poets and even the mystics. As Paul Olson has brilliantly observed,[5] the poet Jiménez constantly moves in a "Circle of Paradox." The first paradox involves the temporal and the eternal; the moment of temporality must be expressed so intensely that it becomes eternal. The second paradox is what Jiménez calls *éstasis dinámico*, or "dynamic ecstasy," that is, spiritual movement which does not cease at the "still point" of ecstasy. The third is found in the juxtaposition of magnitude and brevity; for example, a spark, a wing, a rose are subtly expanded to cosmic dimensions. The fourth, taken from St. John of the Cross, is concentrated in the phrase *la soledad sonora*, the sounding solitude or silence. Finally, there is the difficult paradox of "being in non-being." While Jiménez's intuition of non-being as death almost overwhelmed him in life, as poet he struggled through to a position in which death does not negate the soul. For Jiménez the interplay of these paradoxes provides the basis for the constant tension and limitless expression of his poetry.

In approaching Jiménez's poetry, we can be guided partly by his own analysis, since throughout his career he was constantly preoccupied with his own work and with poetry in general. In 1949, in an important epilogue to *Animal de fondo* (Animal of Depth), he divided his work into three periods: the first, ending around 1909, is characterized by "the ecstasy of love"; the second, ending around 1921, by "avidity for eternity," with God as an "intellectual phenomenon"; and the third, by a "necessity for inner consciousness." A bit later he settled upon two divisions, attempting to underplay any intellectual emphasis, and the major critics have generally agreed upon two periods. The first is characterized by the accepted mutability of all things (which he found encapsulated in Shelley's line "Naught may endure but mutability"); the second by the pursuit of a paradoxical eternalness through temporality by means of a heightened consciousness. From the first to the last, however, Jiménez's poetry ebbs and flows from one pole to the other.

I   *The First Period: The Poet and the Natural World*

In his first period, Jiménez indeed expresses (in his cryptic phrase) the "ecstasy of love," but since he is always surprising, this phrase demands careful analysis. When Juan Ramón Jiménez confidently burst forth into the world of poetry, to his greater glory he was an Adamic figure enchanted by a pristine world, seductive in its innocent beauty. (This is remarkable when we consider that the naturalists and the decadents were already finding the world brutal and rotten.) For Jiménez, the "ecstasy of love" concerns first his fascination with the beauties of nature — the flowers, the fountains, the birds, the moon and stars, the parks and gardens. There exists only the poet's receptive soul and this multifaceted world, and this aesthetic pantheism in some fashion remains alive throughout his career. Only later does he separate woman from nature, woman who is first a dream, briefly a reality, and soon a permanent symbol.

With two books of apprenticeship behind him, Jiménez hit his stride as a poet at the turn of the century, and from this point on his poetic voice was original and unmistakable. He began under the influence of Bécquer, who taught him to listen to the inner voice and to cultivate the brief lyric. For a time he was bedazzled by the surface beauty and sonorous forms of Rubén Darío. He seems to have discovered the symbolist manner in Paul Verlaine, along with the "enclosed garden" approach to nature. In another French poet,

Francis Jammes, he discovered a simple reverence for nature which becomes "Franciscan" in his own poetry. Throughout his first period Jiménez is generally impressionistic in manner, but he is also an incipient symbolist.

Typical is the initial lyric "Dawn" (Alba) of his basic *Tercera antología poética* (Third Anthology of Poetry):

> Se paraba
> la rueda
> de la noche . . .
>   Vagos ángeles malvas
> apagaban las verdes estrellas . . . [6]

> The wheel
> of night
> was slowing down . . .
>   Vague mauve angels
> were putting out the green stars . . .

These tremulous lines are fragmented hendecasyllables and heptasyllables, with soft assonance. This subtle scene of light catches nature at her most indeterminate time, the dawn. Thus her colors are not fixed: the blue of the stars is tinged with the green of earth, the blue sky is shaded into violet from the coming sunlight, and the "mauve angels" are almost an addition of the poet's own subtle emotion. However, the poet is not seeking the pictorial effect, but the *essence* of it, which is stored permanently in his aesthetic consciousness.

Early in his career, Jiménez, still utilizing his impressionistic poetic backdrop, introduces many of his major symbols. For example, in "Parque viejo" the poet at evening is in a deep reverie in the park, where everything seems a "nostalgic dream." Suddenly the natural elements, thus far in stasis, begin a supernatural movement:

> . . . Ramas y hojas se han movido,
> no sé qué turba el misterio:
> de lo espeso de la umbría,
> como nube de incienso,
> surge una rosa fantástica. . . . (10)

> . . . Branches and leaves have begun to move,
> I know not what disturbs the mystery:
> From the deepest part of shadow,

> Like a cloud of incense
> Surges a fantastic rose. . . .

This fantastic rose, in vague feminine form, appears in such intensity that it seems to return the poet's penetrating gaze; then it fades away. This rose is his vision of beauty, or transcendence, capturable only in moments of perfect receptivity. Throughout his first period the rose is presented in all its colors and form as a symbol of natural perfection.

Although in his early *Arias tristes* (Sad Arias) Jiménez is a poet of park and garden, in *Pastorales* (Pastorals) and *Baladas de primavera* (Ballads of Spring), he moves out into the countryside — admittedly the stylized countryside of the pastoral tradition. His ballads of *Pastorals* are a revival of the neoartistic ballad of Lope de Vega in a completely lyric vein. The *Ballads of Spring* reflect the poet in his best singing voice. Typical of his early optimistic pantheism is "Mañana de la Cruz" (Morning of the Cross):

> Dios está azul. La flauta y el tambor
> anuncian ya la cruz de primavera. . . .
>   Vámonos al campo por romero;
> vámonos, vámonos,
> por romero y por amor. (65)

> God wears all blue. The flute and tambourine
> Already announce the cross of spring. . . .
>   Let's away to the country for rosemary,
> Away, away,
> For rosemary and for love!

As an Adamic figure exploring nature, inevitably the poet discovers woman. At first she has no identity — she is confused with the flowers; but when she assumes a seductive form, there begins for this sensuous Andalusian (in contrast with the austere Castilian) a long and dubious struggle for conquest which endures throughout his work. Rather early the poet adopts the Romantic position when he faces a more-or-less real woman; his key lyric is entitled "Desnudos" (We Two Naked) and bears the puzzling epigraph "Goodbyes. Absence. Return." (92). While the beloved plays a sad Beethoven sonata, the two try to understand each other, but she is asking things he "knows nothing of," he is responding with "things

impossible." Naturally the beloved is seeking the normal response of
love; the lover, however, says his goodbye and makes his "Return"
to himself, to his impossible ideals. Another lyric from this same
period is a stunning example of Jiménez's subtle treatment of sensuality. In substance the poet is flagellating his nude beloved as she
flees through the garden:

> Con lilas llenas de agua
> le golpeé las espaldas.
>
> Y toda su carne blanca
> se enjoyó de gotas blancas. (96)
>
> With lilacs dripping with water
> I was beating upon her shoulders.
>
> And all her white nakedness
> Was bejeweled with crystal drops.

In this most delicate of flagellations the beloved dissolves into an
evanescent symbol. That his sensuality was real, however, is proved
by his long *Libros de amor* (Books of Love), a series of fiercely erotic
poems sufficiently explicit for even the wildest decadent. Yet finally
he rejects mere physical union in disgust, calling it "The Ugly."
When a real beloved at last appeared in the person of Zenobia, the
poet predictably transforms their courtship into a masque complete
with the Shakespearean characters Oberon and Titania. Whenever
this delicate poet attempted to grasp a woman, he caressed an idea,
a beloved symbol.

Throughout his first period, Jiménez experimented with most of
the traditional forms of Spanish poetry. After exhausting the popular
forms of ballad and song, he turned to the long and sonorous Alexandrine, the line revived by Darío. It seems that Jiménez utilized the
Alexandrine to express the deeper note of nostalgia which was creep-
ing into his poetry, and what marvels of melody and melancholy he
created with this majestic line! In this period the beauties of nature
are constantly changing and perishing; however, in one of his most
satisfying poems, "La espiga" (The Wheatstalk), this change is for
a noble purpose. First the golden stalk stands in proud beauty in
the fields; then it gives itself back to the earth to create a firmer,

rounder, more golden stalk. In its unquenchable desire for perfection, the stalk becomes a norm for the poet himself:

> Y . . . ¡otra vez a la tierra! Anhelo inestinguible,
> Ante la norma única de la espiga perfecta,
> de una forma suprema, que eleve a lo imposible
> el alma, ¡oh poesía, infinita, áurea, recta! (122)

> And once again to earth! Desire unquenchable,
> Before the unique norm of perfect stalk of wheat,
> Of form supreme, which raises to impossible heights
> My soul — Oh poetry, infinite, golden, erect!

Thus the natural element of the wheatstalk, the poet's soul, and above all his *Obra*, or poetry, are subtly fused into a Platonic perfection.

By 1914, with sixteen years of creating what he later called "flowers of nature" behind him, Jiménez was ready to express himself in the sonnet, that most difficult of forms. The resulting book, *Sonetos espirituales* (Spiritual Sonnets), became for him the culmination of his first period. Indeed, it is one of the outstanding collections of unified sonnets in Spanish poetry. The poet later attempted to change the title to *Intimate Sonnets*, since he realized that there is very little outward movement in his "total longing." Essentially the book records the poet's constant tension in struggling to retain the peak of idealism no sooner reached than lost, his continued progress toward inner perfection, and his "October" position relative to nature.

By common consent the most striking sonnet in the book is "Retorno fugaz" (Fleeting Return), in which the poet explores the power of the "golden moment" (a trite but appropriate phrase which Jiménez never quite uses specifically). This sonnet is a stunning technical achievement in the manipulation of accelerating and decelerating movement, of gliding and staccato rhythms, of interior rhymes. In theme, the sonnet demonstrates (in direct opposite to Proust) the impossibility of recreating the moment in memory.

The poet's total longing and progress toward interior perfection is suspended in a constant tension typical in the sonnet. Surprisingly in the *I-Thou* dialogue of the sonnets, the *Thou* is often the better part of the poet's own nature. For example, in a key sonnet (270) he declares "You always have the branch in readiness/ For the fitting rose"; the title "To My Soul" makes it clear that the poet is in dialogue with himself. Of course he considers himself a worthy subject: his "rose" will be the norm of all roses, his ear the norm of harmony, and his watch as constant as the stars.

Although he has in fact just reached maturity, the poet casts himself against the richness and fullness of nature in autumn. There in his nature the high trees display their "open crowns of gold resplendent" (269); and in the final sonnet the poet's body becomes soul, diffusing itself into this "Enchantment of gold." Such is the beauty of nature in this moment of plenitude that the poet accepts for the time being this destruction as the truth of life.

> En una decadencia de hermosura,
> la vida se desnuda, y resplandece
> a escelsitud de su verdad divina. (275)

> And in a decadence of beauty fair
> Life strips her robes and gleams resplendent
> In loftiness of her one truth divine.

II *The Second Period: Salvation Through the Poetic Symbol*

Around 1915 Jiménez became aware that he had exhausted his first manner, in which the poet in solitude enjoyed the "divine sadness" of a nature in constant change. Thus was born his second period, which he characterized generally as "avidity for eternity." This quest for permanence coincided with his permanent union with Zenobia; the journey across the ocean for the marriage brought him into intimate contact with the sea, not his smiling Mediterranean, but the turbulent and changeable Atlantic. The poet translated these new rhythms into the free verse of what became a major book, *Diario de un poeta reciencasado* (Diary of a Newly Married Poet), which he later declared to be the first important book of free verse in Spanish. In this one instance Jiménez lost his sense of structure, for the long volume contains a useless group of prose sketches of American "materialism," but the poems which trace the tension between poet, sea, and beloved toward final union can easily be extracted.

Even before setting out from Spain the poet senses the magnitude of his journey. Af first the beloved's presence in memory and expectation dominates his heart: "truth without reality yet, how sweet!" (298). One poem specifically compares the beloved with the sea, in the former's favor, although it ends with a surprising maternal image which reveals the poet's nature:

> ¡Tan finos como son tus brazos,
> son más fuertes que el mar!
>   Es de juguete
> el agua, y tú, amor mío, me la muestras,
> cual una madre a un niño la sonrisa
> que conduce a su pecho
> inmenso y dulce. . . . (302)

> As delicate as are your arms,
> they're stronger than the sea!
>   Like a plaything is
> the water, and you, my love, show it to me,
> like a mother's smile that guides
> the child to her breast
> immense and sweet. . . .

Once upon the high sea, however, the poet is stunned with the sea as a gigantic, multiform, living organism. It is significant that for Jiménez the sea is always masculine; it is never the eternal feminine in which he can dissolve himself in refuge. In short, the sea is a symbol *equal to* the poet's own being. Since he is making his journey in February, the dark and stormy sea with its "waves of zinc" communicates a disturbing new awareness to the poet. Its first word is a lugubrious "No," a thousand times repeated (308). Even worse, with great lowering clouds enshrouding its "iron face," the sea conveys that most ominous of words: "Nothingness! The word, here, encounters/ today in me a dwelling place . . ." (308). Thus for the first time the poet reaches a mature awareness of the possibility of annihilation.

When he reaches his destination, his beloved awaits, and this new experience pushes the sea into the background. Naturally the poet, who has lived a long time in his cultivated self-centeredness, suffers agony in adjusting to any sense of sharing; however, in contemplating his sleeping beloved, he finally surprises "the secret of the world's center." By the time of their departure, he has appropriated the beloved into his world, and with this steady refuge, he finds even more perfect freedom to pursue his incessant creation.

> Todo dispuesto ya en su punto,
> para la eternidad. . . . (313)

> Everything is disposed now in its place
> for all eternity. . . .

On the return journey to Spain, now in June, the poet reestablishes contact with the sea, a sea renewed, with colors and beauty and vitality. In his contemplation, the sea actually negates his partial truth of before and replaces it with a more profound truth, a simple "Yes." (327). This yes is not a facile optimism; it means that the poet's consciousness is sufficiently vast to embrace both the light and the dark and yet exist. The sea is therefore infinite in its unceasing movement and power, like the poet's own heart:

> No sé si el mar es, hoy
> — adornado su azul de innumerables espumas — ,
> mi corazón; si mi corazón, hoy
> — adornada su grana de incontables espumas — ,
> es el mar. . . . (331)

> I know not whether the sea is today
> — adorned its blue with innumerable foaming waves —
> my heart; whether my heart today
> — adorned its scarlet with countless foaming waves —
> is the sea. . . .

At times the sea engulfs the poet's consciousness, at times the poet's consciousness engulfs the sea; but both remain "two unique alls, complete and infinite."

It seems that this position of security and confidence should have sustained the poet forever, but for Jiménez back in Spain only his "life" was settled; his soul and poetry were eternally incomplete and in the process of creation. By 1917, moreover, Jiménez was conscious of his stature and potential as a European poet. Having gradually assimilated the European poetic tradition, he now sets out to work at the forefront of that tradition. In general, Jiménez moves toward "pure poetry" in the tradition of Mallarmé, a poetry touched by the intelligence and reduced to symbol, but stripped of the impressionistic, the sensuous, and the sonorous rhymes. Now in full maturity, in the arrogant titles of his major books of the next seven years he emphasizes his confidence: *Eternidades* (Eternities), *Piedra y cielo* (Rock and Sky), *Belleza* (Beauty), and *Poesía* (Poetry). He remains somewhat the same in his infinitely varied projection of idealism, of reaching upward, although now his "roots" are firmly planted in the earth. The new note in his poetry concerns his use of the intelligence in his "avidity for eternity," a perilous pursuit, to be sure.

When he begins afresh, he insists that his poetic word is "not yet made" (337); therefore he calls upon his intelligence to provide that word.

> ¡Inteligencia, dame
> el nombre exacto de las cosas!
> . . . Que mi palabra sea
> la cosa misma,
> creada por mi alma nuevamente. . . . (339)

> Intelligence, give me
> the exact name of things!
> . . . Let my word be
> the thing itself,
> created newly by my soul. . . .

Actually the poet is calling for an efficacious symbol rather than a concept. As was the case with Unamuno, however, Jiménez's emphasis upon the intelligence leads him to "the black thought/ like a nyctalopic bird" (361), which is death. In various poems of subtle definition he attempts to master this dark thought: "Death is only/ looking inward . . ." (479); "Death is our ancient mother,/ our first mother . . ." (526). Like the existentialists, he consoles himself that death is always working with him; and consequently not to be feared (469). More essentially, the poet contemplates utterly recreating and emptying himself in his poetry, so that death will be left with only an empty shell (579).

Only once in this period does the poet completely lose his orientation and mature confidence and hark back to a time anterior to thoughts of death. In the two intensely concentrated lines of "Sur" (South) he utters his cosmic cry of need:

> ¡Nostaljia aguda, infinita,
> terrible, de lo que tengo! (497)

> Nostalgia . . . piercing, infinite,
> terrible, this thing I have!

Since in Spanish *north* is a common symbol for direction or goal in life, the poet's use of the compass point opposite may suggest his radical disorientation. But more likely for Jiménez, *south* means the

Andalusia of his childhood, the Andalusian paradise of innocence, joy, and timeless sea and sky, and his nostalgia for it becomes a permanent theme in his poetry.

In Jiménez's poetry of the second period an intellectual note sometimes prevails; yet we should make it clear that his typical lyric is still one in which he captures a golden moment of transcendence, usually straining upward while solidly rooted — in fact, root and wing are his most expressive contrasting symbols. One of his loveliest lyrics in this vein is "Cuesta arriba" (Uphill), which develops one of his favorite natural symbols.

> ¡Inmenso almendro en flor,
> blanca la copa en el pleno silencio de la luna,
> el tronco negro en la quietud total de la sombra;
> cómo, subiendo por la roca agria a ti,
> me parece que hundes tu troncón
> en las entrañas de mi carne,
> que estrellas con mi alma todo el cielo! (412)

> Immense almond tree in bloom,
> white crown in full silence of the moon,
> black trunk in total quietness of shadow;
> how, as I climb the bitter rock toward you,
> it seems you sink your massive trunk
> in the core of my flesh
> and spangle all the heavens with my soul!

From his youth a prolific poet, it is significant that Jiménez labored from 1923 until 1936 on one of his essential volumes, *La estación total* (The Total Season). The title is of course meaningful: a *season* is a temporal period of growth and decay, but *total* suggests the poet's attempt to fuse all seasons into one, into a difficult eternity. Indeed, in this book Jiménez attempts to synthesize his major themes of his previous poetry, in particular the relation of the natural world to the poet's consciousness and his poetry. He is now "complete in nature," in "golden maturity" (572); his task is to "perpetuate our joyful explosion" and become an "Ardent statue in a peace of dynamism." (571).

In his zeal to eternalize the "golden moment" Jiménez flirts briefly with the idea of eternal recurrence (adapted of course from Nietzsche). Eternity becomes "only that which follows, the same" (570); and the poet expresses this theme lyrically in "Flor que vuelve" (Flower that Returns; 581). But this idea of the eternal return soon proves unsatisfactory to Jiménez, since it seems to suggest a linear movement toward eternity, thereby separating him from others and even from his own past. Therefore in *The Total Season* he begins to emphasize the universal symbol of the circle. In the key poem of the book, all the elements of nature are fused into this circle:

> Las nubes y los árboles se funden
> y el sol les trasparenta su honda paz. . . .
> El cerco universal se va apretando,
> y ya en toda la hora azul no hay más
> que la nube, que el árbol, que la ola,
> síntesis de la gloria cenital.
> El fin está en el centro. Y se ha sentado
> aquí, su sitio fiel, la eternidad.
>   Para esto hemos venido. (Cae todo
> lo otro, que era luz provisional.)
> Y todos los destinos aquí salen . . . (782)

> The clouds and the trees are fused into one,
> and the sun makes them transparent with its deep peace. . . .
> The universal circle is closing in
> and in all the blue hours there are only
> the cloud, the tree, the wave,
> the synthesis of celestial glory.
> The end is in the center. And here eternity
> has found a seat in its faithful place.
>   For this we have come. (All the other,
> which was only provisional light, falls.)
> And all destinies go out from here . . .

Thus the poet unites his own with the common destiny of mankind, but he does it by fusing the universe into the circle of his own consciousness. And, as the lines in parentheses tell us, all his previous poetry is dissolved into this new awareness.

Jiménez joyfully sings this total awareness of the natural world in the lyrics of *The Total Season,* perhaps reaching a peak of intensity in "Criatura afortunada" (Fortunate Creature). This creature is a synthesis of the bird symbol, for it can move in all the natural elements:

> Cantando vas, riendo por el agua,
> por el aire silbando vas, riendo,
> en ronda azul y oro, plata y verde . . .

> Singing you go, laughing through the water,
> You go whistling in the air, laughing,
> in serenade of blue and gold, silver and green . . .

This joyful creature becomes in fact the vitality of natural elements, the lyric poet himself and the transcendence that lurks in and beyond all natural elements.

The masterful synthesis of *The Total Season* ultimately proved unsatisfactory to Jiménez, for the obvious reason that it contains no God.[7] In the early Jiménez, God is only "blue," the blue of the sky and therefore pantheistic, diffused in the beauties of nature. In maturity, God is an intellectual challenge, a creation of the poet's mind. Finally in 1948, Jiménez, again journeying upon the high seas, experienced a mystic encounter with a personal Being ultimately given poetically the name of names, God. The first fruits of this experience were published as *Animal de fondo* (Animal of Depth) in 1949. As he continued to create poems based on this experience (reaching a total of eighty), he ultimately settled upon the title *Dios deseado y deseante* (God Desired and Desiring), although final organization of the book proved to be beyond the aging poet's capabilities.

God Desired and Desiring, clearly in the mystic tradition, is a modern poet's attempt to fuse the aesthetic with the religious in order to achieve a satisfying metaphysical system in a poetical structure. In creating this system, he drew upon his experience with both Oriental and Western philosophy. From his study and translations of the Bengalese poet Tagore, Jiménez developed an interest in Oriental pantheism; his paradoxical expression of "the Many in the One, the One in the Many" often has an Eastern flavor. But Jiménez of course developed in the Western tradition, assimilating the philosophical, religious, and aesthetic ideas which appealed to his own nature. Naturally St. John of the Cross, both a great poet and a mystic, became a model and a challenge. From the opening lines of *God Desired and Desiring,* it is obvious that Jiménez's mysticism is unorthodox.

> Dios del venir, te siento entre mis manos,
> aquí estás enredado conmigo, en lucha hermosa
> de amor. . . .
>
> No eres mi redentor, ni eres mi ejemplo,
> ni mi padre, ni mi hijo, ni mi hermano . . .

eres dios de lo hermoso conseguido,
conciencia mía de lo hermoso. (696)

God becoming, I feel you between my hands,
you are here engaged with me in beautiful struggle
of love. . . .

You are not my redeemer, nor are you my example,
nor my father, nor my son, nor my brother . . .
You are god of beauty achieved,
my consciousness of the beautiful.

Here, since his God is "becoming," he is written with a small letter;
a bit later the poet, of course a "namer," triumphantly puts down
the "name of names achieved": God. Clearly, however, this "God
becoming" is not the eternal Christian God; moreover, he is
emphatically not the Redeemer. This God of "beauty achieved" is
therefore a poet's God, beautiful rather than good.

In developing the space-time dimensions of his God, Jiménez
returns to the traditional symbol of the circle. In the God-oriented
Middle Ages, God is the circle (or the sphere), since this form has a
perfect center and an infinite circumference, thus expressing concentration and infinite space at the same time. Since the
Renaissance, man's individual consciousness has been at the center
of the circle. Jiménez adopts the Renaissance position, but attempts
to superimpose the two circles. His God is "desired" with such intensity that God also becomes "desiring." As "Toward the Radiating
Center" ("Al centro rayeante") makes clear, while the two circles
are constantly superimposed, the center of the poet's consciousness
is the ultimate center. Therefore Jiménez's modern God exists in the
total structure of his poetry; his golden moment in its "dynamic
ecstasy" is equal to the still point of ecstasy of the religious mystics.

While a number of the poems of *God Desired and Desiring* are
conceptual in emphasis, during the course of the book Jiménez
develops many of his beloved symbols in his best lyric manner. In an
outstanding example, he fuses his consciousness with his favorite
color symbol blue, the celestial blue of his Moguer in childhood,
now recaptured (686). In another, as he encounters his God, "All the
clouds are aflame" (680), the clouds being the most ethereal of
solids, bathed in golden light. In still another he concentrates upon
the "glowing coal" to express his mystic experience. Building upon
St. John's "living flame" as both light and warmth, he emphasizes
the glowing coal as a solid also. In a number of lyrics, straining for

utmost concentration, he fuses favorite symbols into one. Perhaps his most expressive is the *Rosa-diamante,* his diamond rose, for the rose is living color, essence, and shape, the diamond perfect shape, permanence, and a receptacle of light.

Jiménez intended *God Desired and Desiring* to be the capstone of his long struggle toward perfect consciousness. As his preliminary title indicates, he was to the end an "Animal of depth," a soul-and-body forever responsive to the colors, sounds, smells, and tastes of the earth. Yet with his symbols he sought to evoke the inner reality in, above, or beyond the senses. In the intensity of the lived moment he attempted to expand the limits of human consciousness and record it in permanent form in his *Obra* as an example for mankind. As a lyric poet this was his "beautiful vocation," his final "ethics through aesthetics."

Juan Ramón Jiménez's position as a lyric poet in Spanish literature has been complicated by his insistence upon seeking purity, universality, and timelessness in his poetry. Somewhat arrogantly, he directed himself toward the "immense minority" (Alas, the only readers of poetry); moreover, he ignored the social and historical realities of his time — even the upheaval of the Civil War. While he enjoyed the adulation of the Generation of '27 for a time, that and succeeding generations have often found his superhuman position to be merely inhuman. As a result, the Spanish literary historians tend to treat him shamefully,[8] but a number of individual critics have studied his poetry with the respect it deserves. This "universal Andalusian" was confident that his divine vocation was to be as pure a lyric poet as possible, and he devoted himself fiercely to that task. In his completeness Jiménez is almost unrivaled in Spanish poetry. He began as an Adamic poet in a fresh world of inexhaustible beauty, determined to express every nuance, every emotion. He mastered all the forms of Spanish poetry: the song, the ballad, the sonorous Alexandrine, the sonnet form, free verse, and the concentrated free verse of "pure poetry." He developed extensively most of the essential symbols of Western poetry with his own emphasis: the sea, the rose, the sun, the tree, the flower, the bird, the cloud, the diamond, the glowing coal, the circle. Admittedly he failed to exploit the ugly: as a man he suffered the ugly and the confused; as a poet, discipline in the quest for beauty was paramount. Jiménez is an outstanding example of the modern poet: since the time of Poe and Baudelaire, given the disintegration of the Christian world view, the poet has been cast adrift to create his own metaphysical system of salvation. Jiménez creates such a system, grounded in a fusion of natural religion and aesthetics and employing the modern preoccupation with the extension of time through heightened consciousness. Moreover, his metaphysical system is properly created in a convincing poetic structure. Surely Jiménez, a deserving recipient of the Nobel Prize, can be meaningfully compared with major European poets such as Yeats and Rilke. Take him for all in all, Juan Ramón Jiménez may well be the greatest lyric poet in Spanish literature.

CHAPTER 5

Backgrounds of the Generation of '27

DURING the 1920s there appeared upon the scene a new group of poets ultimately called the Generation of '27 (some critics prefer Generation of '25), an arbitrary date, since the earliest poets began writing around 1920. Of these poets we have chosen to concentrate upon Pedro Salinas, Jorge Guillén, Gerardo Diego, Federico García Lorca, Rafael Alberti, Vicente Aleixandre, and Luis Cernuda, but of course a number of other worthy poets could be identified, such as José Moreno Villa, Dámaso Alonso, Emilio Prados, and Manuel Altolaguirre. The date 1927 marks specifically the tricentennial of the death of Góngora; these poets undertook successfully a reevaluation of this great baroque poet, and many of them later reveal in a distinctive way his influence. Of course, the major poets of the Generation of '98 were still writing and served, if not as models, as a challenge to excellence. In fact, as Vivanco has firmly declared, the origins of the Generation of '27 can be traced to the work of Juan Ramón Jiménez, not only to his poetry but also to his work as critic in the 1920s.[1] While the influence of Jiménez is largely traditional, in the 1920s, a decade of intense intellectual ferment, many new and varied movements attract and threaten to engulf the new poets for a time: dadaism, ultraism, surrealism, futurism — all threatening either traditional poetry or culture itself. As we have emphasized, Unamuno, Machado, and Jiménez were in certain ways in rebellion against Spanish Catholic tradition, but a number of the poets of the Generation of '27 extended the limits of the rebellion. We should make clear, however, that the Generation of '27 does not make a clean break with the previous one: ultimately the great movement which Jiménez defined as modernism has prevailed throughout the twentieth century in Spain.

It would be difficult to overstate the importance of Jiménez's *Second Poetic Anthology* and his labor as a critic as influences upon the Generation of '27. Published in 1922, the *Anthology* contained ample selections from his mature books of poetry, including *Spiritual Sonnets, Eternities,* and *Rock and Sky.* The purity, concentration, and elegance captivated every member of the Generation of '27, especially in his initial book. Although Salinas, Guillén, and Diego were the three most permanently influenced by Jiménez, all the members of the Generation acknowledged his influence and then successfully struggled to find their own poetic voice. Not content with the example of his poetry alone, Jiménez in the 1920s successfully attracted the collaboration of the newer poets while serving as spiritual director of the journal *Indice.*

In addition to Jiménez's traditional influence, at least one poet of transition between these two generations merits a few words of discussion. In 1920 León Felipe Camino (1884 - 1964), who later dropped the surname Camino, published his *Versos y oraciones de caminante* (Verses and Prayers of a Wayfarer), whose title is extremely significant. The verses of the wayfarer are from Antonio Machado, the prayers from Unamuno; in his wayfarer's life, León Felipe had lived briefly in a dozen little Spanish towns and many countries of Hispanic America. His profoundly human poems explore the brotherhood theme of Machado and the religious theme of Unamuno, but with a simplicity even the brothers with him upon the dusty road can understand. Of the Generation of '27, only Rafael Alberti and later Aleixandre exploit this human and Spanish theme. Therefore, León Felipe serves more fully as a bridge to the contemporary generations, where Unamuno and Machado have become vital influences.

From our vantage point in the 1970s, we can already see that the major poets of the Generation of '27 retained a great deal of Spanish poetic tradition, but for a brief time in the 1920s the various vanguard movements seemed to be making a clean sweep. Since the time of Rousseau, there have been successive waves of rebellion against Western culture, including that of Schopenhauer, the Romantic poets, Nietzsche, the Decadent poets. While the Romantic poets on the formal level rebelled only against stagnated forms, they used poetry itself as a weapon against the middle class. The Decadent poets (of which Darío's modernism was at first an offshoot) retreated into their own ivory tower and often attacked the middle class by ignoring it. After the end of the first World War and in the decade that followed, there is another wave of rebellion, of which we today are still feeling the effects; for a brief time it seemed that this rebellion was going to sweep away poetry and culture. First in point of time is the movement of dadaism, of French origin as were most of these vanguard movements. In addition to their mad personal antics, everyone now remembers the typical dadaist poem: a group of words cut at random from printed matter and pasted together to form a lyric. This attempt to annihilate poetry endured only briefly, and other movements arose.

In Spain, the movement generally called ultraism surged briefly upon the scene, enjoyed a frenetic development, and then withered, leaving a few lasting effects. This movement (under another name) had its origins in France, its chief exponent there being Pierre Reverdy. It was disseminated in Spain by the Chilean poet Vicente Huidobro, who himself claimed paternity of the movement and called it *Creacionismo*. Huidobro developed noble aims for this movement: a poem was to be, not imitation of nature, which satisfied Shakespeare, but unique creation, a being resembling nothing but itself. In America, Archibald MacLeish proclaimed the same goal in his famous line, "A poem should not mean but be." When the young Spanish poets seized upon Huidobro's idea, they rapidly began to formulate doctrines and proclaim manifestos. Among their primary aims was the reduction of poetry to its primordial element: the metaphor. Therefore, the fledgling poets began frantic pursuit of novel metaphors, which they strung together without organization, connecting words, or punctuation in poems. Naturally, traditional poets, such as Unamuno, Machado, and even Jiménez, became anathema to the most radical in this group. Everyone else was "academic" to this group, who considered themselves fresh young children "playing" with the bright new toy of poetry. As one of them (who shall remain anonymous) put it, in what is surely the silliest line of the epoch, "Facing the academic eunuchs, the Ultra poets are deflowering the hymens of the future."[2]

For a brief time the chief *ultraísta* poets took seriously their novel task of creating poetry in a new way, but no complete *ultraísta* poet has survived, and their best efforts have remained in their journals of brief appearance. Perhaps the outstanding books of *ultraísta* poetry were Guillermo de Torre's *Hélices* (Propellers) and Gerardo Diego's *Imagen* (Image) and *Manual de espumas* (Manual of Seafoam). Torre, who thereafter abandoned poetry for criticism, succeeded in his very title in synthesizing ultraism: the spinning airplane propeller, a new object for these poets, is a perfect image of controlled motion, reflected light, and effortless grace. Diego is the only major poet to be seriously affected by ultraism, and we shall later utilize some of his efforts in discussing his poetry. Lorca toyed very briefly with the *ultraísta* manner, but he and the other major poets, while retaining an interest in the cultivation of original metaphor, developed other structures for their poetry.

In this literary atmosphere where the younger poets were avidly pursuing novel image and metaphor, it was almost inevitable that someone should rediscover a poet of Spanish tradition who had achieved the *ultraísta* goal: Don Luis de Góngora. Condemned in Spain by conservative critics such as Menéndez y Pelayo as a "prince of obscurity," Góngora had been rediscovered by (of all people!) Verlaine, and then Rubén Darío, neither of whom understood him. In a spirit of revolt against middle-class values, the generation of Guillén - Lorca set out to reevaluate and reinstate the aristocratic Góngora and in the long run admirably succeeded. Under intense scrutiny, the complicated baroque poems of Góngora turned out to be models of structure and clarity, and above all he represented the cult of metaphor. The Generation of '27 first assembled to commemorate Góngora's tricentennial in Seville in 1927. Even Lorca, not intellectually oriented, ventured into criticism with his essay "The Poetic Image in Don Luis de Góngora," but it remained for Dámaso Alonso, more a critic than a poet in this period, to create the towering criticism which has proved Góngora to be perhaps the greatest European baroque poet. For a time, Lorca, Alberti, and Diego wrote poems in something of the Gongoristic manner, but all the poets of the Generation of '27 learned something from him and translated it into their own original manner.

When the specific preoccupations of ultraism rapidly faded, another movement of much greater importance was already reaching the literary scene: surrealism. Both imply a drastic change in poetic form, but if ultraism is typically playful and unthreatening in theme, surrealism is marked by a grim bellicosity and desperation. Although the word "surrealism" was first used by the French poet Apollinaire in 1918, the movement was most adequately defined by André Bretón in his *Manifesto* of 1924. According to Bretón, in the practice of surrealism, the subject surrenders himself to pure automatism and attempts to reach the products of the unconscious, free of all rational, ethical, or aesthetic preoccupations. The surrealist believes that there exists a superior reality in certain forms of associations formerly neglected; above all, in the domain of dreams and in the play of thought unrestricted by conscious controls. The exploitation of real dreams, of course, evokes Freud's *The Interpretation of Dreams*, published in 1900 but apparently assimilated slowly into European culture. According to Freud, the meaning of a dream is projected through symbols often connected with bodily processes, especially the sexual. Freud himself discovered rich material for his theories in historical subjects like Michaelangelo, and the surrealists rapidly realized that "rebels" such as William Blake, Rimbaud, and Lautréamont were surrealists without being aware of it.

In Spain, naturally, surrealism and Freudianism found hard going, but the younger generation was in an impetuous, rebellious mood, and ultimately the majority of the Generation of '27 were significantly touched by the psychological currents of surrealism and Freudianism. Lorca was surely the first to assimilate something of this movement. In the turbulence of his intimate relation with the painter Salvador Dalí lie the beginnings: while Lorca was a desultory reader, he had a keen intuition for new directions, and Dalí later declared that in the early 1920s Freud's *The Interpretation of Dreams* was one of the "capital discoveries" of his (Dalí's) life.[3] Certain aspects of surrealism, shrewdly disguised, show up in his *Gypsy Ballads* of 1928 — witness the famous "Somnambulistic Ballad." Lorca's *Poet in New York*, written in 1930 but so daring that it was not published in Spain until after his death, is heavily surrealistic in a literary manner. Rafael Alberti, in his *Sobre los ángeles (Concerning the Angels)* of 1929, somewhat timidly approaches the surrealist manner. While this particular book could have been written from Spanish tradition alone, surely Alberti was aware of the new currents, and his minor books immediately following utilize surrealist techniques. Vicente Aleixandre, who admitted reading Freud himself around 1928, utilized him immediately in the prose poems left in "nascent form" of *Pasión de la tierra* (Passion of the Earth), written in 1929, and in his *Espadas como labios* (Swords like Lips), a happily Freudian title, published in 1932. Luis Cernuda, the youngest of the group, adopted the surrealist techniques in his *Los placeres prohibidos* (Prohibited Pleasures), published in 1931. We should emphasize that all these poets insisted that they never utilized the technique of "automatic creation" propounded by Bretón, and, of course, they are correct. It is interesting that Cernuda accused only Aleixandre of employing surrealism, "not as liberation, but as a mask from behind which he could half-say things which he lacked the nerve to say clearly in his work."[4] In fact, this statement applies to all four of these poets. The "things" mentioned involved an attack upon the family itself in various ways; we must add that both Alberti and Aleixandre change positions later, whereas Lorca and Cernuda are rebels to the end. Thus four of our seven poets of the Generation of '27 participated in the rebellion implicit in surrealism, while Salinas, Guillén, and Diego were unaffected in any important way.

On this basis we have somewhat arbitrarily divided the poets of the Generation of '27 into two groups for discussion. Salinas, Diego, and especially Guillén are essentially poets of affirmation, finding the world a possible place in which to exist. On the other hand, Lorca, Alberti, Aleixandre, and Cernuda are essentially uprooted and rebellious, seeing the world as chaotic and tragic. Admittedly this division involves problems: despite his affirmations, Salinas is of tragic outlook; Alberti's rebellion finally becomes mainly political and religious; and Aleixandre emphasizes his "communication" with his people in his second period. All of these poets except Diego reveal at times the strain of having lost the Spanish Catholic faith of their forefathers; in this they are true sons of the Generation of '98.

What is it then that makes this a Generation more than a group of contemporaries by chance living at the same time, since there is a tremendous diversity in their poetry? Perhaps the key was suggested by Jiménez, who in later years lamented that they had fallen into "the limitations of a greater realism."[5] Indeed, this group of poets refused to follow Jiménez in his flights into transcendence; they grounded themselves in the inner realities of this world while retaining the faith of Jiménez and Machado in the efficacy of poetry in reaching this inner reality. As modern poets creating, this Generation is also unified by what Vivanco has called "the exigency of the poem,"[6] but at the same time, the individual triumph over this challenge prevents uniformity. In maturity, each of these poets utilized a pattern of situation, theme, line, image, symbol, and word to achieve a texture intimately his in the finished poem. Since they appeared in a "difficult" period, these poets are complex, at times positively hermetic, and challenge the most dedicated reader, but the fact is that our modern culture demands that the poet create complex structures to project the simplest emotions and themes. The created poem is the poet's goal. And only by presenting these outstanding poems can we hope to demonstrate what Dámaso Alonso has called their "golden" achievement.

CHAPTER 6

Poets of Affirmation:
Salinas, Guillén, Diego

I *Pedro Salinas*

A S the oldest member of the Generation of '27, Pedro Salinas gradually earned a firm, if unspectacular, position as first in the anthologies of poetry covering this period. Moreover, since he matured before Guillén, his *Presagios* (Presages), published in 1923, became the first important book in the new manner of his generation. A traditionalist in both his life and his poetic themes, Salinas was largely untouched by the storms of ultraism and surrealism that swirled around him in the 1920s. Instead, Salinas pursued a type of "pure poetry" characterized by subtle conceits in a language unadorned to the point of dryness. His poetry is perhaps the least sonorous and rhythmical of any of his group. Typical of many of his generation, he began under the influence of Jiménez and ended under that of Unamuno and Machado.

While Unamuno and Machado were poet-professors in Spain, Pedro Salinas is the prototype of the Spanish poet-professor whose profession earned him various positions in many countries.[1] Born in 1891 in Madrid and educated there, he is the only major poet of the century from the capital city. He married Margarita Bonmatí in 1915, and the couple had a son Jaime and a daughter Solita, now the wife of Harvard professor Juan Marichal. Salinas was Reader of Spanish at the Sorbonne in 1914 and at Cambridge in 1922. He taught at the University of Seville, and, with the advent of the Republic in 1933, he helped to found, and became director of, the National University in Santander. In 1936 he came to America and finally established himself at Johns Hopkins University, but he also taught at Middlebury College and the University of Puerto Rico. A respected critic, Salinas in a clear and concise style produced a number of outstanding works, such as *La poesía de Rubén Darío* and

71

Literatura española siglo XX. In fact, Pedro Salinas is an important figure in the growth of Spanish studies in America. He died in 1951 in Boston and is buried in San Juan, near the "Contemplated Sea" of one of his later books.

The poetry of Pedro Salinas, later published by Aguilar in a single modest volume,[2] can be meaningly divided into three periods.[3] In the 1920s, struggling to find his original voice against the influence of Jiménez, he published three books of comparable style and theme: *Presagios* (Presages; 1923), *Seguro azar* (Certain Chance; 1929), and *Fábula y signo* (Fable and Sign; 1931). In his second period he achieved full poetic maturity with two books dedicated entirely to the amorous theme: *La voz a ti debida* (The Voice Owed to You; 1933) and *Razón de amor* (Love's Reason; 1936). In his final period, less unified than the previous ones, the poet reveals the effects of the upheaval of the Spanish Civil War and the sense of impending doom associated with the atomic bomb. In *Todo más claro* (Everything Clearer), including poems written between 1937 and 1947, he records his growing desperation in the face of the insufficiencies of the modern world. In *El Contemplado* (The Contemplated Sea; 1949), inspired by the unceasing creation of the sea off Puerto Rico, he recovered his faith in the generations of man. In his last book, *Confianza* (Confidence), written in the 1940s, Salinas takes final refuge in the salvation of poetry and the brotherhood of poets. Throughout his poetry, despite the particular desolateness of *Everything Clearer*, Salinas is a poet who finds nobility in the spirit of man.

When Salinas initiated his poetic career with *Presages*, despite a recognizable influence of Jiménez, he was already beyond apprenticeship and possessed much of the original manner he was to retain. Throughout his first period Salinas is exploring the possibilities of action and creation, sometimes with a certain ambiguity. As Guillén has suggested, the poet is concerned above all with *soul* — his soul and the soul of things. Naturally, this soul is not moral and religious but involves the heightened awareness of modern consciousness seeking the inner reality of things. Very early Salinas seems to reject the upreaching symbolism of Jiménez and prefers the ground of this earth:

> Suelo. Nada más.
> Suelo. Nada menos.
> Y que te baste con eso.

> Ground. Nothing more.
> Ground. Nothing less.
> And be content with that.

This ground becomes the wider world around him, which he must explore. For Salinas the world is neither the enclosed garden of the early Jiménez nor the grandiose landscape of the Romantics; it is a world prosaic and incomplete until the poet recreates it. Throughout this period the poet is something of a wayfarer, moving from place to place; in his contact with the world the prosaic episodes become materials for his poems, in which he discovers the inner reality he is seeking.

In attempting to embrace the complete world, the poet treats various themes, many of them traditional, but one of the original emphases in Salinas is his fascination with the new objects of the 1920s. This is the period of the Italian Marinetti's futurism, which found an echo in the Spanish poets. For Salinas, the telephone and telegraph, the radiator, the typewriter, and the automobile provided a new world of poetic possibilities, which Jiménez and Machado had sternly rejected. In "Navacerrada, April" the poet has paused at this mountain pass with his "companion," both eager for adventure. The poet's hand presses, not the beloved's hand, but the electric starter of his automobile — and the two become one:

> Alma mía en la tuya
> mecánica; mi fuerza,
> bien medida la tuya,
> justa, doce caballos.

> My soul in yours,
> mechanical; my strength,
> yours well measured,
> sufficient: twelve horsepower.

This tiny stanza illustrates the typical form achieved by Salinas in this period. These lines are heptasyllables, which were used with shorter alternating lines in Renaissance *silvas*. Thus Salinas prefers a cultured form, but it must have that quality which Salinas and Guillén often called *delgadez*, that is, "slenderness." These poets, sometimes with deprecation called "pure poets," strove to trim down, to remove the "fat" typical of earlier poetry. These excesses usually involved trite noun-adjective combinations in form and excessive sentimentality in the theme. As can be seen, Salinas also disdains rhyme and rhythm in the stanza. While it is easy to find it a fault, Salinas cultivated a lean, spare, discursive form throughout much of his poetic career.

In retrospect, it seems that Pedro Salinas in his first period is a poet looking for a major theme. The poet is in almost complete solitude, his limited contact usually being with the things of the world and not with people; yet he exudes the shallow optimism of this period in the potentiality of spirit. In a lyric sweepingly entitled "My Faith" he places his trust neither in the "rose" of art nor the real rose of life, but in what he calls "round/ sure chance," the unlimited potentialities of a soul free toward the future.

In his second period it was fated, declared his intimate friend Guillén, that the poetry of Pedro Salinas would culminate in the theme of love.[4] In his earlier books the amorous theme is approached hesitantly in the form of an "exact beloved," in fact an abstraction, and another beloved compared to the sun-kissed but constantly shifting sands by the seashore. But in his *The Voice Owed to You*, a book-length poem with infinite "variations," Salinas dwells upon the nuances of love with the tenacity of a Petrarch. The phrase of the title is from an eclogue of Garcilaso, and indeed the book carries overtones of the courtly or Neoplatonic love under whose thrall Garcilaso found himself. Moreover, Salinas is following the tradition of the Romantic poet Bécquer, for whom love was a mighty being who occasionally descended to the real world. The poem is an extended contact of an "I" with a "Thou" which has been called a dialogue, but the fact is that this great adventure is elaborated in the consciousness of the poet himself.

Throughout the poem the *tú* wavers between being the beloved and the symbol of love itself, as the opening lines indicate:

> Tú vives siempre en tus actos.
> Con la punta de los dedos
> pulsas el mundo, le arrancas
> auroras, triunfos, colores . . .
> La vida es lo que tú tocas.

> You always live in your acts.
> With the tips of your fingers
> you move the world,
> dawns, triumphs, colors . . .
> Life is what you touch.

Before she comes, the poet is merely a "shadow," dependent entirely upon the grace of love, not his own will:

> Sola, porque ella quiso,
> vino. Tan vertical,
> tan gracia inesperada. . . .
>
> Alone, because she willed it,
> she came. So vertical,
> such unhoped for grace. . . .

In Salinas' bare conceit, this love is "vertical," that is, love as idealized idea; later he will elaborate "love horizontal," where she becomes a human figure.

Gradually, in his simple form, the poet builds to true eloquence in describing the process of love. Naturally love comes as a "lightning flash," bringing destruction of his previous world; even time is destroyed, and the two lovers go back to the "first heartbeat," back before light was, back to the primordial state of "chaos." This overwhelming force proves too much for the poet's immediate experience, and, like Bécquer and Machado before him, he must prolong it "dreaming."

> Tengo que vivirlo dentro,
> Me lo tengo que soñar.
>
> I have to live it inwardly,
> I have to dream it for myself.

And in his dreaming, in his elaboration of consciousness, he strives to reach the essence of love. To express this essence he discovers his most original intuition, the bare pronouns "I" and "Thou."

> Para vivir no quiero
> islas, palacios, torres.
> ¡Qué alegría más alta:
> vivir en los pronombres! . . .
>
> Te quiero pura, libre,
> irreductible: tú . . .
>
> "Yo te quiero, soy yo."

To live I want not
islands, palaces, towers.
Oh joy much higher:
living in the pronouns! . . . .

I love you pure, free,
irreductible: you . . .

"I love you, I am."

Are these pronouns, these "metaphysical entities," perfect abstraction or perfect reality? Surely this is the "essential Thou" Machado searched for so desperately, and the critics have been able to relate Salinas' intuition meaningfully with Martin Buber's important book *I and Thou*.

By a long process the poet enjoys a state which can only be called visionary or mystical, without any religious overtones; for a moment he reaches the "Still point" (in the vein of St. John of the Cross) and then he struggles desperately to sustain his vision. Unsuccessful, of course, his dream becomes a "long farewell" to the beloved. In a very subtle poem, he kisses away the now human tears upon her face; finally, "the material world/ is born when you go away." He is left with his human pain, which he struggles to retain as proof of his experience. In the final poem of *The Voice Owed to You*, the poet is again with his "shadows." But these shadows, the lover and the beloved, "wounded/ by a great nostalgia for material form," are still seeking to become real persons in this world.

Although he successfully projected a powerful vision of love in *The Voice Owed to You*, apparently Salinas wanted to escape from his "dream," his preoccupation with self, and unite with a beloved of flesh and blood. This "project" becomes his second important book of amorous theme, *Love's Reason*. A dream is a true dream, he now declares, when it becomes flesh in "mortal matter." Love is now accepted as temporal, in his subtle reasoning, "a long good-bye that has no end." In an essential poem "Salvation through the Body," the poet stresses the importance of physical being.

Se busca oscuramente sin saberlo
un cuerpo, un cuerpo, un cuerpo.

We go darkly seeking without knowing it,
a body, a body, a body.

And this body only has meaning in relation to its complement:

Porque un cuerpo — lo sabes y lo sé —
sólo está en su pareja.

Because a body — you know it as do I —
only exists in its couple.

For the formulation of this couple, the lovers will offer both body and soul, and thus the two beings united will become the "couple sufficient." The poet accepts these human limitations, what he calls "the tragic truth/ named world, earth, love, destiny."

In his third period, the tremulous "salvation" which Salinas envisioned in the human couple was destroyed by the upheaval of the Spanish Civil War, his emigration to America, and his own advancing age. In a poem (which he hesitated to publish),[5] ominously entitled "Couple, Specter," the poet records his gratitude to the beloved but gradually reveals his preoccupations with man's ultimate destiny. During the years 1937 - 47, confessing his return to the religious and temporal themes of Unamuno and Machado, Salinas produced perhaps his most successful individual poems, which were published under the title *Todo más claro* (Everything Clearer). As in Machado, "clearer" means humanly tragic, not optimistic. The best of these poems utilize the turbulent but meaningless movement of human life in the metropolis. In "Man Along the Shore" (the shore is the sidewalk), the poet focuses upon the imagined meaningless "destinies" of three people passing in their automobiles — a lady rushing to the beauty shop, a business man pursuing his negotiations, a student returning from school. In "Nocturne of the Ads," the poet is in Times Square, meditating upon the optimistic messages upon the lighted billboards. "Lucky Strike" — Where? "Coca Cola. The pause that refreshes." — When? Above all, "White teeth, keep your teeth white." This preoccupation with white teeth suggests to the poet that the teeth are the most enduring part of man's body. In "Zero," the most ambitious poem in the book, Salinas laments the terrible threat of the atomic bomb, which would destroy man's possibilities for living and creation. Salinas compresses the tragic message of *Everything Clearer* in a single powerful line: "The destiny of life is the incomplete."

Despite the negative tone of these poems, Pedro Salinas struggled successfully to preserve a faith in the nobility of man. In 1945, he discovered in the sea off Puerto Rico a positive symbol which provided the inspiration for his book *El Contemplado* (The Contemplated Sea). Since the sea is a masculine symbol for Salinas, it is not refuge but powerful example of eternal movement and unceasing creation. Now clearly under the influence of Guillén, Salinas concentrates upon the act of seeing in the present, the total awareness of light and space. In this book he even attempts to suggest the rhythms of the sea in his lines of alternating length, observable rhythm, and consistent rhymes. In the final poem of the book, "Salvation through Light," the poet submerges a personal immortality in the generations of mankind, eternally contemplating the light upon the moving sea.

Like most of the poets of his century, Salinas in his last book, *Confianza* (Confidence), ultimately took refuge in poetry, in the poet's act of creating in the present. In "Simple Present" he declares: "Neither memories nor presages:/ only the present singing." In the moving lyric "Stop" he focuses upon a raindrop on a leaf, suspended tremulously but tenaciously between life and death. Finally, echoing Bécquer and Guillén, he affirms that while there remains an open window, eyes that face reality, another morning beginning, there will be poetry, and thus life.

Pedro Salinas has earned a solid if unspectacular position as one of the major poets of the Generation of '27. His originality resides in his creation of a poetic style related to the pure poetry of his times, a style characterized by lean and subtle conceits almost mathematical in their precision. For the normal reader he therefore seems to lack the passion of a Lorca or an Aleixandre. Salinas has often been compared (and even paired) with Guillén, and the comparison is apt, but Guillén has gradually overshadowed him in almost every way. Much of Salinas' reputation rests upon his companion books of amorous theme, *The Voice Owed to You* and *Love's Reason*, which have already become modern "classics."[6]

II   *Jorge Guillén*

The Conference at the University of Oklahoma in 1968 dedicated to Jorge Guillén perhaps confirmed his position as the greatest living Spanish poet, above all by emphasizing his international reputation. Guillén had just published his complete works *Aire nuestró* (Our Air) in a beautiful volume in Milan, Italy. The poet must have felt particular satisfaction in being praised for his human warmth, profundity, and universality, expressed in poetry of impeccable form. Early in his career, when in the fashion of the times he was pursuing a "pure" poetry in which the anecdotal was avoided, Guillén received the tag "cold and intellectual," which clung to him for years. Even Antonio Machado, usually a just and generous critic, severely over-emphasized the intellectual aspects of his poetry. The steady growth and interior development of Guillén's poetry gradually earned him a superior position among the many talented poets of his generation. As a modern poet, he has struggled against the normal currents of alienation and despair. If for Robert Frost a poem begins in delight and ends in wisdom, for Jorge Guillén the poem begins in delight and ends in affirmation, an affirmation usually jubilant but sometimes sober.

Like his brother poet Salinas, Guillén has earned his way as a professor, exercising his profession in a host of universities in Spain and many countries of the Western world. Born in 1893 in the old imperial city of Valladolid, and thus a Castilian like Salinas, Guillén earned his degrees at the University of Madrid in 1913 and 1924. He taught at the Sorbonne and at Oxford; in Spain, in Murcia and Seville. From 1940 to 1951 he was a professor at Wellesley, and later he lectured at Harvard, in Mexico City, and in Bogotá. Around 1919, he met Germaine Cahen, a lady of French extraction, in Tregastel in Brittany, at the same time he was beginning his great book of poetry, *Cántico*. In their ideal marriage the couple had a son Claudio, now a professor, and a daughter, Teresa, now married to Harvard professor Stephen Gilman. His wife Germaine died in 1947. After a long period of solitude and adjustment, Guillén married an Italian lady in 1961. During his many years of teaching he wrote one book of criticism, translated as *Language and Poetry,* but throughout his mature life he has devoted himself to the creation of his three books of poetry.

From the beginning Jorge Guillén has been a poet of clarity and order, as the organization of his complete poetry adequately proves. During the first half of his career, he devoted all his energies to the development of *Cántico, Fe de vida* (Canticle, Faith in Life). The first edition, comprising only seventy-five poems, appeared in 1928, a second expanded edition in 1936, a third in 1945; the final edition published in Buenos Aires in 1950 contained 334 poems rigorously organized. Impressed initially by the internal structure of Baudelaire's *Les Fleurs du Mal* and later by Whitman's *Leaves of Grass,* Guillén organized his book in various cyclical and circular movements, such as day toward night, spring toward winter, and youth toward maturity. This period ended, Guillén, undoubtedly influenced by the Spanish Civil War, World War II, and the Cold War, began a second book in counterpoint to *Canticle* reflecting more directly the historical and social realities of our times. This book, called *Clamor* (Outcry), contains three volumes:

Maremágnum (Pandemonium; 1957), *Que van a dar en la mar*
(Down to the Sea; 1960), and *A la altura de la circunstancias* (Keeping Abreast of the Times; 1963). Guillén's final book is a massive
Homenaje (Homage; 1967), in which he generously records his intimate contacts with books and writers from Genesis to the poets he
has influenced. These three books, *Canticle, Outcry,* and *Homage,*
were published under the collective title *Our Air* by Scheiwiller of
Milan in a volume of impressive typography in 1968. Thus Guillén
succeeded, where Jiménez had failed, in imposing order upon the
poetry of his lifetime.

A. *Radiant Affirmation:* Canticle

In the summer of 1919, which he has called his *annus mirabilis,*
Guillén initiated on a beach in Brittany the task of creating *Canticle,*
a project finally concluded in Wellesley, Massachusetts, in 1950.
Thus it is not surprising that from the beginning his poems are universal in theme. Little by little the poet organized his book into five
divisions: "In the Breath of Your Flight," "Appointed Hours,"
"The Bird in the Hand," "Here and Now," and "The Wholeness of
Being." Perhaps the five divisions suggest a circular star with five
points which has the poet at its center. From the beginning also,
Guillén has alternated between the long poem of multiple sections
which elaborate and define his task, and short singing lyrics which
project his controlled jubilation or unusual perceptions.

Canticle opens with a long poem which develops much of
Guillén's philosophy of life and poetry.[7] The poem is entitled "Más
allá" ("Beyond"), but it is clear that for the poet "beyond" means
the things of this world outside himself. The "luminous reality"[8] of
this world is possible through the miracle of light:

> El alma vuelve al cuerpo,
> Se dirige a los ojos
> Y choca. — ¡Luz me invade
> Todo mi ser! ¡Asombro!

> Spirit returns to the body,
> Moves toward my eyes
> And strikes. Light! It invades
> All my being. Wonder!

From the beginning spirit and body are indivisible, but this being
becomes a reality only through intimate contact with the things of
the world.

¡Oh perfección: dependo
Del total más allá,
Dependo de las cosas!

Oh, perfection: I depend
Upon the total beyond,
I depend upon things!

In fact, the reality of the world is such that it "invents" the poet himself:

Soy, más, estoy. Respiro.
Lo profundo es el aire.
La realidad me inventa,
Soy su leyenda. ¡Salve!

I am, nay, I exist. I breathe.
The profound is the air.
Reality invents me,
I am its legend. Hail!

In the simple words of this stanza Guillén frees himself from the solipsistic morass in which many modern poets (such as Jiménez) have floundered. Of great importance is the untranslatable difference between *soy* and *estoy*. In Spanish these verbs *ser* and *estar* both mean "to be"; *ser* means essence in the abstract, while *estar* means to be in concrete presence in place and time. Therefore for Guillén existence in relation to the things of the world is reality.

Of first importance is the reality of the world outside the poet; then through rapt attention to that world the poet adds something more, the poetic word. As Guillén concludes firmly in the poem "Además" ("Besides"), "Everything becomes a marvel by addition" ("Todo es prodigio por añadidura"). Such is the intensity of Guillén's attention to, and appreciation for, the common, everyday object that he can find life pulsing in a table, as in "Naturaleza viva," which can be translated as "Unstill Life."[9]

¡Tablero de la mesa
Que, tan exactamente
Raso nivel, mantiene
Resuelto en una idea
Su plano: puro, sabio,
Mental para los ojos
Mentales! . . .

Surface of a table top
Which so precisely
Smooth and level sustains
Resolved in an idea
Its plane: pure, wise,
Mental for mental eyes!

This penetrating visual attention is confirmed by the poet's touch, and in the "rich heaviness" of the wood he senses the walnut tree whence it came. In the grains and whorls of the wood remain the vigor, the concentrated power, and life of the forest itself, so that in the poem the inert object comes to life, at the same time retaining the planes of its artistic form.

Perhaps the lyric which most adequately represents the originality, the delicate radiance, and the controlled jubilation of Guillén in his singing manner is "Cima de la delicia" ("Summit of Delight").

¡Cima de la delicia!
Todo en el aire es pájaro.
Se cierne lo inmediato
Resuelto en lejanía.

¡Hueste de esbeltas fuerzas!
¡Qué alacridad de mozo
En el espacio airoso,
Henchido de presencia! . . .

Más, todavía más.
Hacia el sol, en volandas
La plenitud se escapa.
¡Ya sólo sé cantar!

Summit of delight!
Everything in air is bird.
The immediate hovers,
Resolved in distances.

Host of slender forces!
What alacrity of boy
Upon the buoyant space
Bursting with presence . . .

More, always more.
Toward the sun, on wings

>Plenitude is escaping.
>Now I can only sing!

This is an example of "pure" poetry, although "not too pure" Guillén always insisted. Characteristic are the subtle definition of the first line and the sweeping totality of the metaphor of the bird in the second. Contrary to the usual manner of projecting a specific bird, the pure poet seeks intense concentration of materials. Of course, this sweeping kind of metaphor can only be used once. The "slender" forces of the second stanza are another subtlety of the pure poets. All the poetic resources are purified toward slenderness, with a deliberate attempt to avoid either leanness or fragility. The poetic lines themselves are slender and artistic heptasyllables. Moreover, Guillén demonstrates here his mastery of the subtle assonance, or vowel rhyme, of Spanish. Whereas in popular poetry assonance is customary in the even lines, Guillén assonates these stanzas *a b b a*, and changes the assonance from stanza to stanza.

Another much-quoted lyric which demonstrates Guillén's mastery of image and line is "Primavera delgada" ("Slender Spring"), which begins as a morning river scene, delicate but without focus:

>Cuando el espacio sin perfil resume
>   Con una nube
>Su vasta indecisión a la deriva,
>   —¿Dónde la orilla?) — ...

>When space without profile resumes
>   With a cloud
>Its vast indecision set adrift ...
>   Where the shore?

Gently this river curves back upon itself (suggesting motion without going anywhere); the poplars along the shore shimmer in the morning light. Finally the poet focuses sharply and crystallizes spring itself at the point of the dripping oars of the boatmen:

>¡Primavera delgada entre los remos
>   De los barqueros!

>Slender spring between the oars
>   Of the boatmen!

In this image the poet seems to capture the essence of spring in the delicate thread of translucent water which rises from the returning oars. Moreover, we now understand that the rhyming couplets with lines of alternating length perhaps suggest the rhythm of the long pull stroke and shorter return stroke of the oars. And the lyric, which begins as a static scene, teems with the energy of spring at the end.

As a poet of order and form, Guillén, in addition to creating his own stanzaic forms, revived and mastered certain traditional ones, especially the *décima* of the Golden Age drama and poetry. This rhyming stanza of ten short lines, like a miniature sonnet, demands concentration and technical skill on the part of the poet. With it Guillén created at least a dozen excellent poems, often focusing upon humble objects, such as a glass of water, a favorite armchair, an equestrian statue. Perhaps the finest of his *décimas* of broad theme is "Perfección" ("Perfection").

> Queda curvo el firmamento,
> Compacto azul, sobre el día.
> Es el redondeamiento
> Del esplendor: mediodía.
> Todo es cúpula. Reposa,
> Central sin querer, la rosa,
> A un sol en cenit sujeta.
> Y tanto se da el presente
> Que el pie caminante siente
> La integridad del planeta.

> The firmament is curved,
> Compact blue, over the day.
> It's the rounded form
> Of splendor: high noon.
> Everything is dome. The rose
> At center of all reposes,
> Held by the sun at zenith.
> And the present so prevails
> That wayfaring foot perceives
> The planet's integrity.

This compact verse is impossible to translate into English form without sacrificing detail. Guillén condenses the enclosing curve of the firmament in the metaphor of the dome; without further reduction the sun's light is focused upon the rose, traditional symbol of perfection. By focusing upon the rose he brings the light down to the immediate world. Such is the intensity of this static (or eternal) moment that the foot (both firmly tactile and symbolic of movement and change) feels the wholeness of things. It is characteristic of

Guillén that he bravely chooses the shadowless light of high noon; most poets prefer the softer light of other hours, which conceals the imperfections of the world.

As a poet who needs intimate contact with the things of this world for the completion of his own identity, naturally Guillén in his *Canticle* soon discovers that most enticing of objects, the beloved. As a poet of love Guillén is a striking exception in Spain. Of course he inherited the deeply rooted Renaissance tradition of Petrarchan, courtly, or Neoplatonic love, in which the poetic fusion of the real and the symbolic values of woman is rarely achieved. In truth, the philosophers of love (that is, all poets) usually preached that the presence of woman made "real" love impossible. In fact, in a typical poet like Garcilaso, his love drove him deeper into solitude. Jiménez, in the twentieth century, continually rushed out toward woman, then promptly "destroyed" her reality by flying off into symbolism. Given the awesome reticence of the Spaniard, before Guillén there is hardly a serious poem in Spanish upon the act of love.

In *Canticle* Guillén creates a series of monumental poems which glorify the act of love between man and woman and its deep significance for him and for life. His first major poem of love is "Salvación de la primavera" ("Springtime Salvation"), composed in nine short but carefully constructed sections — and thus typical of his major efforts. Perhaps since Guillén was a mature man when he began to write, in his poetry there is no adolescent love of daydreams and ineffable longing. "Springtime Salvation" begins with the presence of the nude beloved in clear light (this love has nothing to hide) and in a setting of daily objects. There is no magic, only a heightened reality. As the passion of the lovers intensifies, the poet's "slender" verses control any drift toward the lascivious or the trite:

> Henos aquí. Tan próximos,
> ¡Qué oscura es nuestra voz!
> La carne expresa más.
> Somos nuestra expresión.

> Behold us here. How intimate,
> How dark is our voice!
> The flesh expresses more.
> We are our own expression.

The poet traces the normal course of love to its climax, to the moment of union. And is this union infinite? No, he declares, love "is enraptured in its own limits"; afterward lover and beloved return to serenity. This "perfection of an instant" is sufficient of itself; the reality of the act needs no further symbolic meaning. Therefore when toward the end of the poem the poet calls the beloved "river of adventure," "window toward the diaphanous" and "high noon in its rose," she is still of this earth.

After " Springtime Salvation" Guillén returns to the theme of love in "Anillo" ("Ring"). Now in summer, love is mature and seasoned, but ever fresh, ever adventurous. The ring is the wedding ring, but it is also the perfect circle and therefore the symbol of the wholeness of life. For this poem of mature love Guillén chooses a classical stanza of traditional hendecasyllables with full rhyme. Again the lovers are together in their normal setting while outside the summer afternoon sun reigns in its potency. Again the complete experience of the passionate union is traced as before, but such is Guillén's talent that hardly a nuance of the earlier poem is repeated. At climax, "Everything is potency in astonished cry"; and indeed, as the ring closes, this love becomes "Love in creation, in flower, in son." Such is the power of this love that it throws out a challenge to death:

¡Sea la tarde para el sol! La Tierra
No girará con trabazón más fuerte.
En torno a un alma el círculo se cierra.
¿Por vencida te das ahora, Muerte?

Let afternoon be for the sun. For life discloses
No stronger bond upon this spinning earth.
Around the spirit the circle firmly closes.
Do you declare yourself now conquered, Death?

Guillén's final statement in *Canticle* on the love of man and woman is found in "Los fieles amantes" ("The Faithful Lovers"). Their love, which bloomed symbolically in the light of morning and matured in the warmth of afternoon, has now reached its "night":

Noche mucho más noche: el amor es ya un hecho.
¡Qué diario Infinito sobre el lecho
De una pasión: costumbre rodeada de arcano!
¡Oh noche, más oscura en nuestros brazos!

Night more than night: love is now a deed . . .
What daily Infinitude upon the bed

> Of a passion: custom encircled in secret!
> Oh night, oh darkest night in our arms!

This "dark night" is of course that of St. John of the Cross, and we must remember that in his complex symbol, the night is dark, not in foreboding, but in absolute contrast with the light in his heart. Moreover, here Guillén declares that love is the reality of daily custom suffused with intimacy, against the Neoplatonic tradition prevailing in Western poetry that love is a unique vision, which the poor poet is forever afterward seeking to recapture. Guillén's most sweeping definition of love is found in the poem "Ring": "Amor es siempre vida, sólo vida" ("Love is always life, only life").

Toward the center of *Canticle* Guillén in maturity placed a short cycle of sonnets, that most demanding of forms. The sonnets in general recapitulate his essential themes in a traditional form; clearly the poet is testing his wings, as did Jiménez at midpoint in his career, against the poets of the past, such as Lope de Vega and Quevedo. His first sonnet reexpresses the importance of casting off the solipsism of night and waking up at the light of dawn, which "invents" the world: "Todo lo inventa el rayo de la aurora" ("Everything is invented by the beam of dawn"). He also continues his struggle to live grounded in reality, against the seduction of the "dream," to which Machado and Unamuno surrendered.

> ¡Realidad, realidad, no me abandones
> Para soñar mejor el hondo sueño!
>
> Reality, reality, abandon me not,
> That I may better dream the deep dream!

There appears, however, one important new theme, the one which inevitably must strike the poet grounded in this world. In "Muerte a lo lejos" ("Death at a Distance")[10] he records the thought, but the urgent thing is now the "mature fruit" of his poetry, and he calmly adopts the stoic philosophy exemplified in Quevedo that death (symbolized in the whitewashed walls of the Spanish cemetery) is the law of life.

> El muro cano
> Va a imponerme su ley, no su accidente.
>
> The gray-white wall
> Will impose its law upon me, not accident.

Of great importance is the major poem "Vida extrema" ("Utmost Life"), in which Guillén exalts the transformation of life at the fullest into poetry. The poet develops the disciplined "conduct" of attention, concentration upon the world to such a point that matter itself reveals its "substantive magic." And for the poet, "Everything is condensed toward the world." But this transforming miracle of world into poetry demands the "great Yes," the going out toward the world and its possibilities. For his concluding line Guillén appropriates one of the richest words of the Christian faith to enrich his own meaning: "¡Gracia de vida extrema, poesía!" ("Grace of life at the fullest, poetry!").

The title *Canticle* suggests an emphasis upon the song of affirmation and exaltation, but of course Guillén is aware of evil and disharmony in the world. In the earlier poems the poet typically emerges from formless darkness into light and clarity, while in the later poems evil threatens more insistently. But the poet holds evil and destruction in abeyance by an act of will. In fact, there are no old men, no winter in the cycle of *Canticle*. When in the final poem the poet meets evil face to face he recognizes its power but refuses to yield. His refuge is the open window upon the world and his disciplined concentration upon its hidden possibilities.

No brief discussion can adequately convey the richness and variety of *Canticle*. The theme is ever the same: richness discovered in the normal things and acts of living. In these poems of radiant affirmation Guillén's passion for life, expressed with control and originality, always burns brightly. The lyrics of *Canticle* are universal in theme, and therefore little dependent upon time and place. Like any great lyric poet Guillén is untranslatable, but as long as Spanish is spoken this book of poetry should remain a treasure.

B. *The Poet in Time and Circumstance:* Outcry

With *Canticle* completed and with the accumulation of years, Guillén finally acknowledged the terrible pressures of our times in the trilogy later called *Outcry*. In the first volume, entitled *Maremágnum* (Pandemonium; 1957), occasionally there are poems of his usual affirmation, but in general these serve to provide contrast with the poems of confusion, darkness, and threatened optimism. In the first important poem, "Tren con sol naciente" (Train at Sunrise), while as usual darkness goes toward light, dawn comes in a hard and bitter struggle, and it reveals through the dirty windows of the train a group of weary faces, each in an alien setting. The train, itself "swift pandemonium" and a symbol of homelessness, hurtles its passengers toward unknown destinies. One of the major poems of this book is "Potencia de Pérez" ("Power of Pérez"), a scathing attack against the dictator ruling Guillén's Spain. Pérez is a Mister Nobody in spirit (though of course not in power), and surrounding him is a Chorus of bureaucrats, police, party hacks, and even the clergy. For Guillén the future is closed; he can only record his bitter outcry in solidarity with fellow poets such as Cernuda and Alberti.

In *Pandemonium* Guillén introduces for him a new form of expression which he calls "Tréboles," or "Clovers." These gnomic poems of a single stanza of three or four short lines came to him apparently by way of Antonio Machado, who had adapted the form from the Rabbi Sem Tob, Campoamor, and the Andalusian *copla*. Guillén's *Tréboles* serve him for his usual affirmation, for the expression of pained skepticism, and often for the accumulated wisdom of his years.

> Somos, juntos en flaqueza,
> Hombres de posible acuerdo.
> Cuando en el error me pierdo
> La fraternidad empieza.

> We're men of possible accord
> United by our sins;
> When I in error lose my way
> Brotherhood begins.

Throughout *Pandemonium* the prevailing theme is confusion, disorder, crime, and the threat of death and destruction, with occasional poems of affirmation in counterpoint. Gone are the joy and triumph of *Canticle*, even in the matter of expression, for a number of the most negative poems are cast in a form resembling prose. In the final peom, a sonnet, entitled "Sueño común" (The Dream in Common), the poet joins his fellow man in a common sleep which is a resigned escape from the pain of life. For a poet whose faith is the act of living, sleep is also a suspended death. His final apostrophe is to his own tired body, threatened perhaps by oblivion:

> Cuerpo tendido: todo en paz te mueres
> Negando con tu noche tantos males,
> Rumbo provisional hacia la nada.

Body laid out: with all in peace you expire,
Denying with your night so many wrongs,
Provisional journey toward nothingness.

If *Pandemonium* is a book of confusion and outrage, the second volume of *Outcry, Que van a dar en la mar* (Down to the Sea), is deeply elegiac in tone. Of course, the title emphasizes a well-known line from Jorge Manrique's serene elegy upon the death of his father and the passing of all things of this world. In *Down to the Sea* Guillén becomes a "poet in time" in the fullest sense of Machado's phrase; his emphasis is upon time and memory, his struggle is to recover his "ordinary equilibrium." In the initial poem the poet projects himself in the *persona* of Lazarus, first striving to return from the grave. The poet's initial experience with death can perhaps be traced to the death of the beloved wife; his problem is whether to accept the Christian faith with its hope in eternal life or to return to this world, his world. With the help of humanity (exemplified by Mary and Martha) he returns to the light and air of this world, pleading humble ignorance of any concept of "Eternal Life." In "Viviendo" (Living) he has recovered his equilibrium and his calm acceptance of this life:

Acepto
Mi condición humana. . . .
El mundo es más que el hombre.

I accept
My human condition. . . .
The world is more than man.

In perhaps the major section of *Down to the Sea*, entitled simply *In Memoriam*, Guillén records in moving detail the presence of the beloved wife, the growth of their love and family, and his situation after her death. Destiny, says the poet, brought them together in Brittany; they built a life together despite constant changes of scene. With the beloved gone and become memory, Guillén stubbornly insists upon his philosophy of the reality of this world and refuses to make their love "symbolic" of anything: "Fue real, y por eso amor supremo . . ." ("Real it was, and therefore love supreme . . ."). In seeking a symbol for the beloved wife, Guillén settles upon a synthetic one which becomes the title of an essential sonnet: "Rosa estrellada" (Star-Spangled Rose). The rose has vitality, color, and perfection of form; the star intensifies light upon the rose, and at the same time suggests rays toward the center of a circle. Whereas for Jiménez rose and star symbolize perfection *beyond* this world, for Guillén they symbolize real woman.

Beginning in *Canticle* and continuing throughout his career, Guillén utilizes the sonnet to record his pilgrim's progress through the passing years. Two such sonnets appear in this book. In the first, "Del trascurso" (Time's Course), the poet looks from his vantage point in the present toward his past with such deep perspective that naturally the future seems foreshortened:

> Ante los ojos, mientras, el futuro
> Se me adelgaza, delicadamente,
> Más difícil, más frágil, más escaso.

> Meanwhile before my eyes the coming years
> Spin out their thinning filament delicately,
> More difficult, more fragile, more tenuous.

In "El Descaminado" (Astray) he is fighting the dark thoughts of insomnia, yearning for the light and balance which were always his.

> Quiero la luz humilde que ilumina
> Cuerpo y alma en un ser, en uno solo.
> Mi equilibrio ordinario es mi gran arte.

> I want that humble light which illuminates
> Both soul and body in a single Being.
> My ordinary equilibrium is my great art.

In the third volume of *Outcry*, *A la altura de las circunstancias* (Keeping Abreast of the Times; 1963), Guillén struggles manfully (but like so many others somewhat unsuccessfully) to keep abreast of the frightening sixties. His opening sonnet, significantly entitled "A pique" (On the Brink) focuses grimly upon the rats (not the people) vainly seeking to escape from their foundering ship. One gloomy poem predicts the end of the world, unless man achieves "patience, intrauterine patience." The threat of the hydrogen bomb evokes "El asesino del planeta" (The Assassin of the Planet); that assassin will probably be a well-dressed technocrat suddenly invested with unlimited power. Guillén fails (as did his friend Salinas and everyone else) to convey the moral and physical horror of world destruction in a merely verbal structure.

Guillén is on more solid ground when he concentrates upon his own personal stance. He makes final peace with his mother country in "Despertar español" (Spanish Awakening); through his poetic word he reaffirms his pact with the "white wall" which is Spain. In "Dimisión de Sancho" (Demotion of Sancho) Guillén through this beloved character humbly accepts his own solid place in life. Sancho, after a brief stint as governor of an island, ultimately realizes what he is and returns to his place and his task in his own village. Guillén's final personal sonnet, entitled "Ars vivendi," is complex in its extensions of meaning and simple in expression. This title surges in contrast to the typical phrase "Ars moriendi," which emphasizes dying instead of living, and evokes a magnificent sonnet of Quevedo, who in his Christian philosophy and baroque expression sees each successive moment of this life as a perpetual "dying." Guillén indeed feels his mortality, as one of his most moving lines expresses it: "Ay, Dios mío, me sé mortal de veras" ("Oh Lord, I know I'm truly mortal"). But even at seventy years of age he reiterates his philosophy that life is a succession of moments lived intensely, and the poet's task is to capture and exalt these moments of the act of living.

C. *A Meeting of Lives:* Homage

Toward the end of his career Guillén organized an immense collection of poetry of circumstance accumulated over the years, along with a surprising number of new poems which record the still-rich experiences of his autumn years. Even Guillén's incidental poetry possesses a quality of form and originality few poets could equal at their best, but the reader can relax and muse upon a great poet's intimate contact with consecrated figures alive to him through literature. Guillén's first extensive collection of poems are "On the Margin" of books which have generally stimulated his admiration and occasionally his wrath. One tender lyric focuses upon the Brownings, Elizabeth and Robert, in Italy, striving to translate their dreams into a real love lived day by day. But another excoriates the Marquis of Sade, since Guillén had no patience with the abnormal. There is an ample collection of translations, the earlier ones of poets who influenced him, such as Paul Valéry, and the later ones of poets in whom he recognized a kindred spirit, such as Wallace Stevens. At the center of *Homage* Guillén proudly placed a collection of amorous lyrics which trace the birth and growth and final triumph of his autumn love for "Silvia." Unlike Machado, whose autumn love for Guiomar dissolved into dream, Guillén tenderly achieves his love in the flesh and sings his simple gratitude.

In the later sections the aging poet prepares to take his leave without tears or didactic lessons. There are his usual sculptured sonnets of pilgrim's progress, with a "slender" thread of life stretching out before him. In "El cuento de nunca acabar" (The Story that Has no End) he takes final leave of his son, passing on the torch of "adventure." "Dying," he reaffirms with utter simplicity, "is only sad"; being, living are absolute. With his passion for order and unity, Guillén rounds off both his life and poetry:

> Hemos llegado al fin y yo inauguro,
> Triste, mi paz: la obra está completa.
>
> At last we have arrived and I inaugurate
> In sadness my final peace: the work is done.

Despite an early prejudice against an overemphasized intellectual tendency in his poetry, Jorge Guillén has gradually achieved recognition as one of the greatest poets of the twentieth century. From the beginning Guillén firmly situated his being in a reality dependent upon the persons and things of this world for fulfillment, and he has always written poetry in vital affirmation of that existence. For him, being is living in time and place in intimate contact with the world: life as its own justification. This is, in the awesome phrase of our century, "phenomenological existentialism," but Guillén's glory is that his poetry of luminous reality and radiant affirmation creates this world in convincing unity and imperishable form. His *Canticle,* one of the half-dozen best books of poetry in Spanish literature, preserves in original form the sound, nuance, and manner of the "slender" or pure poetry of our century, along with an impressive variety of traditional forms. Even his *Homage* is unique among books of this type of poetry "on the margin." Certainly Guillén can be (and he has been) censured for not being a popular poet; but what major poet's poetry has ever been really popular? Like Jiménez in this, Guillén courted the "immense minority," that is, the diligent reader willing to educate himself in poetry. His major competitor in this generation, García Lorca, bedazzled many even at the popular level, but Lorca himself had to confess that his poetry was grossly misunderstood. Guillén is a noble poet whose best poetry is written in time and place, yet timeless in form and theme, and surely it will preserve its freshness and vitality as long as Spanish is a living language.

III *Gerardo Diego*

Of all the members of this generation, Gerado Diego is perhaps the outstanding example of versatility and virtuosity. Like Lorca and Alberti blessed with raw poetic talent, he has displayed it in an amazing variety, from the verbal extravagances of ultraism to the rigid form of the medieval "four-fold way," with its quadruple rhymes. As he has perhaps wistfully confessed, he was not born with the bristling passion of an Unamuno or the modern charisma of a Lorca, and he has thus remained in their shadow; leading a quiet and exemplary life in a chaotic century, he has devoted himself to largely traditional themes, sometimes disguised in extravagant form. In his fecundity and variety, he has disconcerted the critics by failing to establish a controlling theme in his poetry, as did Unamuno and Guillén. But the body of his published poetry is of a consistently high quality, given his grace of form.

Born in Santander in 1896, the youngest of a large family, Diego began his advanced schooling in a religious institute in Deusto and completed his doctorate in liberal arts in Madrid.[11] Like Machado he spent several solitary years teaching in institutes in the provincial towns of Soria and Gijón, finally earning a like position in Madrid. In 1934, already 38, he married one of his students, Germaine Marin, of French ancestry, and the couple has produced a large family. Very early Diego devoted himself to the vanguard currents of ultraism and creationism; toward 1927 he founded the literary journals *Carmen* and *Lola* which promoted these movements. As a critic he conceived and produced a still-respected anthology of the poets of his generation. As a final mark of his traditionalism, Diego was inducted into the Royal Academy in 1948, and in his autumn years he has become (along with Aleixandre) the grand old man of Spanish letters in present-day Spain.

From the beginning of his career he has alternated persistently between the vanguard and the solidly traditional, so that followers of both movements have at times questioned his sincerity. But Diego has tenaciously defended his position: "I am not responsible if I am attracted simultaneously to . . . tradition and the future; if the new art enchants me and the old sends me into ecstacy. . . ."[12] As a youngster, naturally he gravitated first toward the vanguard movements which following World War I began to pervade Spain. Stimulated by friendship with Vicente Huidobro, the Chilean who founded creationism, and Juan Larrea, a practitioner of this kind of poetry, Diego dedicated himself to creating books of poetry following this manner. In Spain, the vanguard movement has typically been called ultraism, but Diego has insisted that he has followed creationism, specifically because the creationists pursued a novel objective poetry, while the ultraists concerned themselves excessively with destroying tradition.

Gerardo Diego produced two early books of vanguard poetry, *Imagen* (Image; 1929) and *Manual de espumas* (Manual of Seafoam; 1922), almost the only survivals of this ephemeral movement, and he has occasionally returned to this manner throughout his career. Although typically these poems are too long to be presented adequately, the tiny lyric "Guitar" serves well as a first example:

> Habrá un silencio verde
> todo hecho de guitarras destrenzadas
>
> La guitarra es un pozo
> con viento en vez de agua
>
> There'll be a green silence
> all composed of unbraided guitars
>
> The guitar is a well
> with wind instead of water

Although smacking a bit of Lorca's imitation of the Andalusian *cante jondo*, the poem contains the novel image and surprising contrasts of the manner. The silence is strangely green, since this color suggests vitality; there is silence because the guitars are "unbraided," that is, the broken strings are flying loose like hair flying free. As a container the guitar is like a well of life, but here it is filled with wind and produces only a sigh. As a result the form and sound of the guitar are "unrealized" in the novel images.

Many of Diego's poems of creationism utilize typography so that the lines present a meaningful shape upon the page, a technique as old as the Greeks but revived for this period by the French poet Apollinaire. A blatant example is the short poem "Ajedrez" (Chess). On the left side of the page, in the poet's heart "the piano has cavities," that is his song is decayed; on the right side, however,

"from the parachutes canticles still rain." The conclusion projects
these contrasting states of emotion visually:

La muerte	y la vida
me	están
jugando	al ajedrez
Death	and life
with	me
are playing	at chess

Clearly the two chess opponents are facing each other across the
page.

In our grim epoch this "playful" attitude seems a luxury almost
criminal, but Diego follows the typical manner of the 1920s as the
creator in solitude, seeking his novel metaphors which are poetry
and nothing else. In that day this type of poetry perplexed and infuriated the traditionalists. But we now understand that the
meanings are as old as poetry: the poet in his solitude, bursting with
emotions and yearnings, is attempting to make contact with the
alien and confusing world outside, usually without success. Consequently, a street lamp is a "wound," a word is an "explosive
magnolia," time tastes of "chloroform"; outside, the poet is a
"shepherd of boulevards"; inside he "smokes" his verses. While at
first Diego uses this cryptic manner without punctuation and connecting words for poetry of isolation, as the years pass he employs it
for human poetry which is autobiographical, and often with serious
theme. For example, as late as 1955, he uses the vanguard manner to
approach freshly the ancient theme of man's responsibility in the
poem "El hombro" (Shoulder).

> Sentí en el hombro un dulce peso
> un fardo ligerísimo como violín de pensamiento
> un fardo inmenso como nube . . .
> La creación entera se redondea en hombro
>
> I felt upon my shoulder a sweet weight
> lightest of burdens like violin of thought
> burden immense like cloud . . .
> Entire creation is rounded on shoulder

Even during his years of intense interest in ultraism and
creationism, however, Gerardo Diego gradually mastered the

traditional forms of Spanish poetry, and he often published his books in alternation between vanguard and traditional forms and manner. His early *El romancero de la novia* (Ballads for the Sweetheart), naturally in ballad form, elicited an encouraging word from Antonio Machado. Machado's Soria as a poetic theme was appropriated by Diego during his stay there, and this Spanish theme has persisted over the years in his poetry. His tremulous ballad of presence, time, and memory devoted to the Duero river has justly earned a place in the anthologies:

> Río Duero, Río Duero,
> nadie a acompañarte baja,
> nadie se detiene a oír,
> tu eterna estrofa de agua.

> Duero River, Duero River,
>   No one to your shore belongs;
> No one pauses now to hear
>   Your eternal water song.

Another consecrated anthology piece is his reworked sonnet which captures the essence of the ancient cypress in the gardens of the monastery at Silos in Old Castile. This cypress, which, unlike the sprawling American cypress, is conical in shape, provides the poet with a series of metaphors of upward thrust; it is a "fountain jet of shadow and dream" a "mast of solitude," an "arrow of hope." Above all, the sonnet prefigures the poet's return to the faith of his forefathers.

Of his many books of poetry, both vanguard and traditional, perhaps the critics have chosen as the outstanding single book his *Alondra de verdad* (Lark of Truth), written before 1936 but not published until 1941.[13] This collection of sonnets demonstrates from the first his mastery of this difficult form. There are sonnets of love, in a fashion reminiscent of courtly love, sonnets on the Spanish landscape, in the manner of Unamuno, and even a religious sonnet entitled "Grace," couched in evasive metaphor. Despite the brillance of the individual sonnets, however, no reigning theme emerges clearly and forcefully.

For many years Gerardo Diego himself, a poet of versatility and variety, apparently could not establish a central theme in his poetry, nor could the critics. He has been read in his *First Anthology*, published in 1947, and in his *Second Anthology*, published in 1967, both of which offer only brief selections from his many books. Moreover, Diego has surprisingly continued to delay the publication of his complete or even collected works. In 1965, however, he published a solid thematic anthology entitled *Poesía amorosa* (Amorous Poetry) which may well reveal his controlling theme.[14] He has declared, in a single verse, that he was not attuned to the clamorous rebellions of our times: "Yo nací para amar, y a nadie odio" ("For I was born to love; no one I hate"). In the preface to *Amorous Poetry* he reveals his own affinities in his selection of the great amorous poets of the past. With a passing nod to Garcilaso, he chooses from the Golden Age Lope de Vega, Quevedo, and the lesser-known Villamediana; from later poets he exalts Bécquer and Salinas. But his central focus is clearly upon Lope, since one of his important sonnets concludes: "Porque Lope soy yo, ¿no lo sabías?" ("For I am Lope — you say you knew it not?"). Although it is surprising that he should equate himself with a volcanic figure such as Lope, Lope represents specifically a Golden Age poet who enjoyed the Neoplatonic vision of love, but more importantly, he lived with the loves of his inspiration. And (unlike Petrarch and Quevedo, for example) Lope was too much of this earth to abjure his human love when he turned to the divine.

In his life and poetry Gerardo Diego attempts this most difficult of fusions, the transformation of human loves into a love both metaphysical and religious, or Christian. Diego (like Lope) has enjoyed, not the unique experience of the Neoplatonic poets, but a continuing vision of love centered in the various aspects of the Eternal Feminine. His first love awakened in him the awareness of the beloved "other" in the world and a desire to transform himself into something better, and he emerged from this initial "encounter" a being "all new."[15] After many years the poet discovered his essential and enduring love in the beloved who became his wife; in his *La Sorpresa* (The Surprise; 1941) he consecrated this experience in delicate and chaste lyrics which became a surprise gift for the beloved. This love assumes a permanence clearly religious in "Nuestro huerto" (Our Garden), where Diego suspends his customary originality and repeats the most intimate lines for a Catholic: "Ave María,/ gratia plena."

Diego's vision of love anchored in the Eternal Feminine is completed in his devotion to the mother and the sister, recorded in the circumstantial poems of *Mi Santander, mi cuna, mi palabra* (My Santander, My Cradle, My Word). Moreover, in his intimate contact with the work of the Mexican nun Sor Juana Inés de la Cruz, he discovered in her famous poem "Primer sueño" (First Dream) a theme essential to his own vision. In his "Second Dream," through his intimate contact with her, the poet truly understands that the second dream is the "dream of human love toward the divine." The very purity of the nun's life and devotion have made it possible for him to realize his own unworthiness and thus to be receptive to divine grace.

In full maturity, Diego, unable by nature to respond to the themes of our times, has returned to the Golden Age for both theme and manner. Still fortified by his deepening visions of love, he reworks in his own original expression the typical manner of Lope de Vega. In a series of sonnets and songs to "Viola" (Violante being one of Lope's muses) the poet recreates the joys and pains and glories of love, pristine and relived. Two of these sonnets are of critical importance, as Diego himself has suggested. His favorite "Tuya" (Yours), a verbal *tour de force* largely untranslatable, projects the essential theme of the completed cycle of his love. While in Renaissance poetry the beloved is typically disdainful and unreachable, here the beloved herself responds with the "yours," even spelling the word musically for emphasis. In "Mano en el sol" (Hand in the Sun), the beloved's right hand held up to the light is transfigured by the "Christian sun" into the eternal; that is, the poet sustains his belief in the resurrection of the flesh.

The capstone poem is the concluding one which provides the title for the book *Amor solo* (Love Alone). The poet has now ascended beyond his human loves, beyond even Hope and Faith to the ultimate Love which is God:

> Sólo el Amor me guía.
> Sólo el Amor y no ya la Esperanza,
> Sólo el Amor y ni la Fe siquiera.
> El Amor solo.

> Only Love leads me on.
> Only Love and now no longer Hope,
> Only Love and now not even Faith.
> Love alone.

Thus in a life of quiet dignity, Diego has managed to sustain a vision of human love both moral and licit (in contrast to Lope's) and to pursue it through the adventure of poetry to a condition of possible beatitude, an anchoring in the Catholic faith. In our time it is no mean feat.

Given his solid traditionality in theme and often in form over against flights into vanguardism mainly in form, Gerardo Diego has at times been guardedly accused of insincerity, a charge he has vehemently resisted. His quiet optimism, his assimilation of the best of all worlds, has perhaps seemed timid and traditional when contrasted with the rebelliousness of a Lorca or the modern metaphysical system of Jiménez. Our condensed presentation of Diego's traditional theme should not obscure the fact that he has developed this theme and related ones with remarkable versatility and originality. He is probably the most talented sonneteer since Quevedo. He has provided the most unified collection of poetry of the brief movement known as ultraism or creationism. And, as an example of his versatility, it is he (not Lorca or Alberti) who has most expansively pursued the Spanish theme of the bullfight in his *La suerte o la muerte* (Grace or Death). The publication of his complete works, which now includes more than twenty volumes of poetry, should put the final seal upon his reputation as a versatile, dedicated, and prolific poet, for like Guillén he has been blessed with the grace of expression even in his most circumstantial lyrics.

CHAPTER 7

Poets Uprooted and Rebellious:
Lorca, Alberti, Aleixandre, Cernuda

I *Federico Garcia Lorca*

OF all the twentieth-century Spanish figures Federico García Lorca has gradually achieved the widest reputation, especially outside Spain, so that people who know only a half-dozen Spanish names can recognize his. He was born with the *gracia* ("grace") of Andalusia, of the "dark" Andalusia of Granada and Córdoba. For his own generation he was always the *niño*, the "child," a term which suggests charm, originality, and spontaneity. But for the mature Spaniard, the term also implied a lack of responsibility toward profession, family, and class. In maturity he became a follower of Whitman in demanding total personal liberty for the individual and for the oppressed group — the poor, the gypsy, the Negro, the homosexual. He was an early example of the contemporary youth of class and privilege who attacks his own class while continuing to sponge off it. He possessed in abundance that modern charisma which in our day makes a celebrity, but his appeal was based upon his genius for assimilating the essential themes of his times and projecting them in original works. Thus Lorca became one of the symbols of our turbulent and unsettled times, and his poetry captures these tensions and confusions. His tragic and untimely death, which is still a subject of morbid fascination and controversy,[1] put the final seal upon his reputation.

Lorca (who preferred, contrary to tradition, to emphasize his mother's name) was born in that smiling plain called the Vega near Granada in 1898 into a family of well-to-do landowners.[2] A precocious lad but a predictably indifferent pupil, he was pressured into the customary study of Law. Escaping to Madrid in 1919, he became a perennial student without goals or curriculum among the group of bright young men in the Residence of Students, a group in-

101

cluding Salvador Dalí, Luis Buñuel, Alberti, and others. Lorca plunged into this exciting literary atmosphere and began to develop his talents as a poet and dramatist. During these years he developed an intimate relation with Dalí, but the two budding geniuses soon reached a parting of the ways, Lorca going to New York, Dalí to Paris. During the 1930s Lorca dedicated himself intensely to the drama, working with a traveling company called La Barraca and staging his major plays such as *Blood Wedding* and *Yerma*. On the eve of the Civil War he returned to Granada and was caught up in the deadly struggle between the contending forces. Arrested by the controlling Falangist forces, in the confusion of the moment he was executed at Víznar outside Granada on the morning of August 19, 1936. His death provoked a national and international furor which has not entirely subsided yet.

A. The Gypsy Ballads

In retrospect, most of Lorca's earlier poetry seems to be a preparation for his *Romancero gitano (Gypsy Ballads)*, the book which earned him his international reputation.[3] After his initial *Libro de poemas* (Book of Poems), a book of apprenticeship, Lorca in the 1920s began to explore the various literary currents swirling around him in Madrid. From the beginning he felt the attraction of both the traditional and the vanguard, and from the beginning he displayed a genius for assimilating the vital elements in both traditions. Stimulated by his Andalusian experience and his collaboration with the composer Manuel de Falla, Lorca first explored the traditional in his *Poema del cante jondo* (which we know as flamenco), begun in 1921 but not published until 1931. Lorca's brilliance manifests itself in these Andalusian songs, insistently tragic in a woeful key. His central theme is that of the "vanishing rider," a horseman on his way to a "distant and lonely" Córdoba which he never reaches. Lorca of course exploits Andalusian themes to perfection in the *Gypsy Ballads*.

When we pass from Lorca's earlier books of poetry to the *Gypsy Ballads*, we soon become conscious of a quickening, an urgency, a power that builds without slackening throughout the book. The predominant theme of the *Gyspy Ballads* concerns the presence and outpouring of a vitalism both primitive and modern. This vitalism is the life-force, for Lorca an earth-force residing in the blood itself and transmitted through the five senses. This force is primitive in that the gypsy character follows his passions in natural freedom, oblivious to social or cultural restrictions. It is modern in that it is much like Freud's ideas of the libido, an all-consuming sexual urge seeking an undifferentiated sex object. Thus the specific theme of many ballads is the omnipresence of the sexual instincts, not love but mere physical passion, passion normal and prohibited, passion repressed and incestuous. Since this passion is constantly being thwarted it often turns into aggression, and aggression leads to death. This pattern of passion, frustration, and psychic death follows the emphases of psychology in the 1920s. This passion also becomes embroiled with religion in some "historical" ballads. Lorca himself discounted the thematic importance of the gypsy and insisted that the *Gypsy Ballads* was an "Andalusian tableau," which for him involved sensuality, religious fervor, and persecution. In Lorca's tragic vision no Freudian "adjustment" to life is possible; life is consumed in its own frenzy of passion, beyond social or divine aid or condemnation.

As the title *Gypsy Ballads* indicates, Lorca after earlier experimentation finally settled on the form of the Spanish ballad, a medieval form repolished by Lope de Vega and Góngora in the Golden Age and revived in the twentieth century by the Machados and Jiménez. Lorca's ballad, with octosyllables and continuing assonance, is completely traditional in metrical pattern; what distinguishes Lorca's style, later imitated briefly as the "Lorquian manner," involves his brilliant and imaginative metaphor, a technique learned partly from ultraism and partly from Góngora. These metaphors often depend upon a displacement of forces or a fusing of actions; a typical example is the lines "The beaks of the eager cockerels/ Dig, seeking out the dawn," where the food being dug is replaced by dawn itself, during the time this action occurs.

The first of the ballads, "Romance de la luna, luna" ("Ballad of the Moon"), plunges us at once into Lorca's mysterious and difficult world. The protagonist of the ballad is his *niño*, or "little lad," who has seen the moon "in her bustled skirt of white" descend to the forge where he is dreaming. The moon therefore seems to be a mother figure, but in the key lines that follow, "the moon displays, lascivious and pure, her breasts of hard tin." The boy, fascinated by the figure, is strangely attracted and repelled, and finally she takes him away through the sky, leaving the gypsies of the village wailing. In a mythological sense this can be interpreted as a dreaming lad who refuses to participate in the real world and escapes into the fairyland regions of the shimmering moon. But it is also an ingenious example of Freud's Oedipal complex, a theory which aroused heated controversy in the 1920s. The mother-figure's breasts are both "lascivious and pure"; therefore the child feels a sexual attraction which he must attempt to reject because the mother must be pure. Since in Lorca no "adjustment" is possible, the lad follows his primary instincts. This ballad is typical of Lorca's ambiguous fusion of the modern and the primitive.

In four of the ballads the protagonist is a woman, reacting in every case to the primary sexual instincts. In "Preciosa and the Air," this innocent maiden is frighteningly awakened to the pansexuality of the world when a St. Christopher figure as a wind-giant attacks her. In "The Gypsy Nun" (an ironic title since gypsies are rarely nuns) the young nun is struggling to transmute her sexual passions into the flowers upon the piece she is embroidering. For his "Thamar and Amnon" Lorca recreates the fierce biblical story of this princess' incestuous love for her brother Amnon. Of all this group, the outstanding one is the "Ballad of the Dark Anguish," in which Soledad Montoya comes storming down from the mountain, seeking "her joy and her person":

> Cobre amarillo, su carne,
> huele a caballo y a sombra.
> Yunques ahumados sus pechos,
> gimen canciones redondas.

> Her flesh of yellowed copper smells
>   Of shadow and stallion strong;
> The smoke-hued anvils of her breasts
>   Are moaning rounded songs.

This firebrand of sexuality, typical of the twentieth century, is a transparent double for the poet himself, who in sympathetic dialogue with her counsels her to "bathe her body with water of morning larks," that is, to transmute her passion into song.

While in the ballads just discussed the imagery is sometimes shocking (or was, in Lorca's time), it was when Lorca began to project male characters that his intentions approached the prohibited in traditional Spain. Therefore, he used his poetic skills of evasion by creating mystery so effectively that his meaning has remained obscure for many readers. His Antoñito el Camborio (subject of two gripping ballads), a pretty, self-centered lad, is ultimately killed by his own clan because of his deviation from the norms of gypsy masculinity. Of all the ballads, Lorca's favorite was the "Somnambulistic Ballad," whose mysterious first stanza the whole Spanish world has memorized:

> Verde que te quiero verde.
> Verde viento. Verdes ramas.
> El barco sobre el mar
> y el caballo en la montaña.

> Green, green the color, bewitching green,
>   Green winds, green tinted fountain;
> Boat upon a far-off sea,
>   Stallion on the mountain.

In this Freudian dream sequence (as the title suggests) a wounded lad pursued by the forces of the law returns to his home, where a mysterious She (Is she woman, Death, a gypsy lass?) awaits, "her eyes of frozen silver." A *compadre,* an Andalusian buddy, also awaits, and the two lads discuss their plight. Then the two companions climb up beyond the balustrade, up to the "stairway of the moon." The "She" becomes a gypsy girl who has drowned herself in the cistern. When the civil guard arrives, the two companions have disappeared into their ideal domain of perfect freedom and art, beyond the persecution of the world. It is instructive to compare this ballad with Whitman's fantasy of the "twenty-eight lads" and with A. E. Housman's ballad "Hell's Gate." Lorca later loved to recite this ballad as his masterpiece, for him the essence of poetry itself.

In his "Ballad of the Spanish Civil Guard" Lorca offers his finest projection of aggression and persecution. In the contemporary fashion, this guard, painted entirely in black, represents destruction and evil, not protection and justice. The ominous guard swoops down upon the innocent and joyful gypsy camp, where a religious celebration is going on. With their sabers they slash the cardboard figures of the saints and the flesh of the fleeing gypsies and destroy the camp completely, finally leaving in a "tunnel of silence." Then in the last stanza Lorca seizes the impact of the long poem and focuses the turmoil, persecution, and anguish in his own face.

In summary, the *Gypsy Ballads* is a book which reveals Federico García Lorca's unsurpassed imagination in transmuting the materials of Andalusian popular tradition into an expression of his own tragic vision of life. While it lacks spiritual values, the book projects with white-hot intensity the primal life-force or earth-force (often expressed through the sexual), which is continually seeking expression. But this life-force, which encounters frustration, repression, and defeat, is always thwarted by social and religious forces and even the nature of the universe itself. Therefore almost all the ballads end in real or psychic death, with no alleviation offered or expected. As a result, Lorca has been cast as a *poeta maldito,* a poet who accepts life as accursed, in the tradition of Baudelaire and later poets.[4] In English literature, Housman's *A Shropshire Lad* provides a meaningful comparison in both theme and form. But for all these poets the poetry which springs from this tragic situation abides. Lorca's *Gypsy Ballads,* which has gone through more than a dozen editions in Spanish, has attained the glory of being assimilated into the stream of modern European literature.

B. Poet in New York *as an Example of the Rebirth Archetype*

When Lorca's *Poet in New York* appeared in 1940 (he had dared to publish only a few of its poems in his lifetime), most of his readers and critics were perplexed and disconcerted. The success of his *Gypsy Ballads* had stamped him as a popular singer of ballads and champion of the gypsies, a stereotype against which he fought bitterly. *Poet in New York* was obviously a book utterly different; it was written in the general manner of surrealism, in a free verse of varied and unfamiliar rhythms, with a clang of symbols and a profusion of extravagant images difficult to decipher. With the advantage of critical distance, we now know that Lorca's book was not an isolated phenomenon but an example of the sudden veering toward the surrealistic mode which occurred toward 1930 in Spain. Lorca's *Poet in New York* indeed projects a chaos of rebellion, alienation, and despair, but so solid is the general structure of the book that it strongly fits the pattern which critic Maud Bodkin established as the Rebirth Archetype. The psychologist Carl Jung discovered and developed the pattern of the archetype in his study of major figures in different times and places. Typically the subject finds himself in a state of compulsion, in total frustration without hope or aim, but with intense efforts he fights through to transcendence and is reborn to a new purpose. Maud Bodkin employs Coleridge's well-known *Rime of the Ancient Mariner* as a model, and it is easy to establish certain essential comparisons between Coleridge's poem and Lorca's.

Lorca's *Poet in New York* begins at a strong negative point in the death-rebirth cycle. Interestingly, Lorca himself analyzed his book as having an interrelated double theme: a crisis of the poet and a crisis of the City. Common to both is a condition of suffering, of seething death in life. It is a mistake to suppose, as many have done, that the City caused the poet's crisis. As the initial poem of the book makes clear, the poet brought his crisis with him, for he has been "assassinated by heaven," between the forces of "serpent and crystal," that is, malevolence and light. In the epigraph of the poem, quoted from his brother poet Cernuda ("Fury color of love, love color of oblivion"), Lorca subtly suggests that his unrequited love for the comrade has been the cause of his despair and depression. This theme, as a torturing obsession and as a lingering memory, persists throughout the book.

In his initial contact with the City, the poet discovers one group with which he can deeply empathize: the Negroes of Harlem. For him, the Negro possesses the vital life-force equal to his own, a life-force "without history," that is, a force for expression in the here and now, unaffected by fears of the past or responsibility for the future. But in his famous "Ode to the King of Harlem," he projects an even more salient characteristic: the murderous rage pent up in the heart of the black man because of centuries of oppression.

> La sangre no tiene puertas en vuestra noche boca arriba.
> No hay rubor. Sangre furiosa por debajo de las pieles.
> Viva en la espina del puñal y en el pecho de los paisajes.
>
> Blood has no outlets in your night face upward.
> There is no blush. But blood is raging under the skin,
> live in the thorn of a dagger and the breast of a landscape.

At a time before it became apparent to everyone, the poet in his own suffering intuits the Negro's true feelings and prophesies his coming rebellion.

The poet's raging attitude toward the teeming masses of New York is one of rejection and repulsion. In his "Landscape of the Vomiting Multitudes" he employs the subhuman imagery of the surrealists (or the Freudians) to convey his horror of the seething masses. His central focus falls upon a fat lady at Coney Island, who "turns the suffering octopus inside out." His "Landscape of the Urinating Multitudes" continues this theme of violent rejection and alienation.

Toward the center of the book the poet develops his central crisis and his reaction to it with grim irony and evasion. In the tiny poem

"Murder," the surface details present a stabbing, but the specific imagery forces us to interpret this as a homosexual "murder." The poem "Christmas on the Hudson" is a peculiar reexpression of the Fall, a fall from a state of innocence into the practices of the flesh. While a spectral chorus sings "Alleluia" the poor *niño* is stretched out by the sailors; afterward he is left in a void, a "world alone," with the "fable" of his innocence destroyed. In "Dreamless City," subtitled with obvious irony "Brooklyn Bridge Nocturne," there surges an awareness of guilt with an emphasis upon the pressure of the flesh. A philosophical section of the poem negates the theme of Calderón's famous play *Life Is a Dream*:

No es sueño la vida. ¡Alerta! ¡Alerta! ¡Alerta!
Nos caemos por las escaleras para comer la tierra húmeda . . .
Pero no hay olvido, ni sueño;
carne viva. . . .

Life is no dream. Beware, beware, beware!
We fall down from the stairways to eat the humid earth . . .
But there is neither forgetfulness nor dream:
Living flesh. . . .

For the Catholic Calderón this life is a dream, but eternal life follows; for the modern poet reality is "eating the humid earth" of physical passion. And for the time being even his power to transmute his physical vitality into poetry has deserted him.

From the depressing atmosphere of the City, the poet retires or escapes to the rural countryside, with the symbolic suggestion of surcease and recovery in the world of nature. Perhaps the turning point in the poet's struggle is suggested in another difficult poem, "Moon and Panorama of the Insects," subtitled "Poem of Love." The two contending forces are the moon (which is ultimately rejected), associated with the memory of the face of the lover, and the attraction of the teeming insects. Here the symbolic meaning of the insects is not clarified, but in a related poem (strangely left out of *Poet in New York*)[5] the poet expresses himself clearly: "I ask the holy Mother of God/ to give me the pure lights of the insects,/ creatures who love without eyes. . . ." Thus he receives a lesson in humility from these humble creatures, and from this point he begins his rebirth by looking outward in compassion toward all beings. It is significant that Coleridge's Ancient Mariner begins his rebirth when he becomes aware of the "slimy water snakes."

When the poet returns to the City, he has recovered his direction and developed a commanding and prophetic voice. As modern hero, he has even conceived a program of action, whose essence is concentrated in two major odes, the "Cry Toward Rome" and the "Ode to Walt Whitman." In the "Cry Toward Rome" the poet climbs symbolically to the tower of the Chrysler Building and directs a challenge toward the seat of Western culture, attacking the older generation of spiritual and cultural leaders. In the "Ode to Walt Whitman," the poet seeks to establish a select society coexisting within the larger one, but of course outside it. For the Spanish poet, Whitman is a symbol of a "classic" who is also new; he is a second "Adam of blood," a new Adam, beginning, centering, and ending in himself. For him, Whitman represents the fullest expression of physical and artistic vitality, of that tragic "burning of the blood" of the individual self, outside the Christian tradition of family and promised immortality. The poet envisions a select society of comrades, the "pure" and the "classic" united in physical, spiritual, and artistic brotherhood, which would presumably coexist with normal society. As a final challenge to the Establishment he would have a young Negro boy announce the "arrival of the Kingdom of the wheatstalk," this symbol (like Whitman's calamus) being both phallic and representative of the earth-force.

With his rebirth complete, his program for himself and the larger group conceived and delivered, the poet has only to suggest the destination of his journey. The concluding poems indicate that he, like Coleridge's Ancient Mariner, is also "a sadder but a wiser man"; moreover, given our turbulent modern period, he is necessarily a figure of modern irony. In his "return to civilization" (having been in the great city of New York, let us remember) he takes off for Santiago of Cuba on his way home. This choice of Santiago of course suggests a wider meaning; in former times to "go to Santiago" was to go to Santiago de Compostela, a focus of Western Christian civilization. His choice of Santiago of Cuba and his focus upon the vital "primitive" elements there emphasize his faith in the promise of neoprimitivism in its manifold forms. Therefore it is not surprising that Lorca has become one of the heroes of the various youth-oriented liberal movements of contemporary times, with their emphasis upon the primitive and even the barbarian, in uncompromising conflict with traditional Western culture.

Poet in New York is an intense, painful, prophetic book, worthy of being included among the finest examples of the alienation of spirit in modern man. Strongly within the surrealist tradition, it can be meaningful compared to Lautréamont's *Chants of Maldoror* and Rimbaud's *A Season in Hell,* both written earlier but achieving their importance during the surrealist period. It is also an achievement in poetic form, in a powerful free verse of marked contrast with the form of the *Gypsy Ballads.* Most of the poems of *Poet in New York* are frighteningly personal at one level; yet, as we have emphasized, such is Lorca's genius for transforming his personal experience into a broader statement that the book becomes a prophetic analysis of the immediate future, especially as concerns the revolution of the Negro, the continued assaults against social and religious institutions, and exaltation of the primitive — all this of course under the aegis of total liberty for the individual. For *Poet in New York* can be meaningful interpreted in the broadest context of the Rebirth Archetype, in which his chaotic theme and form stand in stark contrast to his general and timeless structure, and indeed the book crystallizes the dream of our times that total liberty for all will bring a rebirth of civilization itself.

C. *The Later Poetry*

After returning to Spain from New York, Lorca began perhaps as early as 1931 the creation of the lyrics that became the slim volume *Diván del Tamarit* (Divan of Tamarit), finally published in 1940. The *Diván* (Arabic word for gathering, by extension, anthology) and the Tamarit (a family estate near Granada) in the title suggest a specific evocation of the Moorish or Arabic civilization. The theme of the *Divan of Tamarit* centers around the anguish of the memory of love and the poet's present despair, which he is struggling to transmute into poetry. The poet's voice has at times become disembodied; his universe is one of presentiment and nostalgia, of dark instincts and faded passions. In the key initial lyric "Ghazal of Unforeseen Love," Lorca sketches in imagery partly Oriental and partly surrealistic his attraction to the comrade-lover:

> Nadie comprendía el perfume
> de la oscura magnolia de tu vientre.
> Nadie sabía que martizabas
> un colibrí de amor entre los dientes.

> No one understood the perfume
> Of your belly's dark magnolia.
> No one knew that you were martyring
> A hummingbird of love between your teeth.

This strange image of the "hummingbird of love" was briefly shared by the comrades. And the image of the dark magnolia (of course normally a great flower brilliantly white) conveys all the suggestion of *oscuro* for him. It is his dark night of passion, dark of isolation and oblivion, and his lost or destroyed collection of *Sonetos del amor oscuro*, his development of the "new Adam," that is, Adam without Eve. In the poem he goes on to emphasize that he sought to make his love eternal, but the broken form of the last stanza indicates it was not to be.

In the typical and moving "Qasida of the Lad Wounded by Water" Lorca returns to his symbolic well and the walls of his Granada, a Granada of loneliness. The "wounded lad" weeps moaningly, his head "drowned with hoar-frost"; around him the waters of the pools and cisterns and fountains are not sustaining life but are "brandishing swords," swords which threaten the very life of the poet. Face to face with his anguish, he falls extended along the earth, the waters of his agony curving over him, wanting to die his death "by great mouthfuls," a death of cosmic frustration.

The *Divan of Tamarit* is simply one of the saddest volumes in all of Spanish poetry. Not so well known as his two major books, it nevertheless completes his tragic vision of life in an intensely personal vein, drawing upon the rich field of suggestion of the Arabicoandalusian culture and cast in a mature form containing elements of both his free verse and his neopopular rhythms. Moreover, the *Diván del Tamarit* is frighteningly prophetic in that it presents the poet's ultimate isolation and psychic death in his Granada, which he loved (and sometimes hated) like a true Spaniard. In his Granada, said Antonio Machado disconsolately in a moving poem, he found his real death in confusion and loneliness.

It is fitting that Lorca's last major poem should be his *Llanto por Ignacio Sánchez Mejías (Lament for the Death of a Bullfighter)*, for in this noble elegy he succeeded in interweaving significant aspects of the Spanish tradition of the bullfight while demonstrating his own personal and poetic qualities. More importantly, perhaps, with his genius for poetic synthesis, he successfully projected an outstanding example of the existential hero of our times. Shortly after his friend Sánchez Mejías was mortally gored in Manzanares on August 11, 1934, Lorca composed his *Lament* in four impressive movements of varied forms, generally in the tradition of the classical elegy, but with an insistent modern emphasis upon death as annihilation. In the first section, "The Goring and Death," the poet gives way to horror and deep despair at the sudden presence of death. A pattern

is achieved in the alternating of longer lines, which carry the imagery, with the octosyllabic refrain "At five in the afternoon," which
creates the effect of a monotonous dirge. Finally, "Death put eggs in
the wound" of the terrible horn, and the bull, now a symbol of death
itself, "was bellowing in his forehead." Even though this scene is
short, Lorca is at his most powerful in the projection of foreboding
and death.

In the second section, "The Spilled Blood," the poet gradually
forces himself to turn away from the blood upon the sand to focus
upon the bullfighter in his moments of triumph. The bullfighter
creates his form of plastic art in a dramatic moment in the presence
of death itself, and the living Ignacio faced this challenge with
courage and grace:

> No hubo príncipe en Sevilla
> que comparárselo pueda,
> ni espada como su espada
> ni carazón tan de veras.

> There never was a Sevillian prince,
>   Who could with him compare;
> Never a sword like his sword
>   Nor ever heart so true.

In the formal third section, "The Body Laid Out," the poet
woefully traces the final dissolution of the body into the earth.
Naturally, then, in the final section "Absent Spirit" nothing is left
but to sing in praise of the vanished hero. And what does the poet
sing? "I sing his profile and his grace," responds Lorca. Against
tradition, this seems such a fragile thing, the total profile, the image
of the bullfighter, in plastic beauty of form and grace in the
presence of death itself. But such is an essential quality of the existential hero, in whom the facing up to the fragility and imper-
manence of life is accepted and extolled as man's ultimate courage.
Lorca's *Lament for the Death of a Bullfighter* therefore becomes an
outstanding testament of our modern times.

As a poet (and as a dramatist as well) Federico García Lorca has
achieved an enviable reputation, not only in the Hispanic countries,
but also in the rest of the Western World. In his person and in his
poetry he captured the imagination of his own generation and the
succeeding ones as a significant voice of our times. His *Gypsy
Ballads*, in imperishable form, reflect in masterful fashion the vital,

popular, and primitive emphases of our century, in conflict with the traditional values of Western culture. His *Poet in New York,* in both theme and form, exemplifies the turbulence, alienation, and individualism of the twentieth century; yet, in its positive aspects as a Rebirth Archetype it exalts total liberty for everyone, including the submerged minorities. In Spain Lorca's poetic influence has not been profound, for he has been considered an original who is impossible to imitate, while in Spanish America he helped to stimulate the swing to popular forms and native traditions. Lorca's poetry is insistently tragic in tone; yet such is his vitality that he has often been received for his valiant joy. Among Spanish poets, in spiritual kinship he is closest to Aleixandre and Cernuda, as both recognized; Aleixandre portrayed him movingly as a vulnerable creature who enjoyed life and love in constant peril of destruction. Surprisingly, he is like Guillén in that both are vitalists who extol this world and underplay transcendence; however, his dark and tragic vitalism stands in marked contrast to Guillén's radiant affirmation. For Lorca, as for his whole Generation, the imaginative leap into poetry resulting in the finished poem was the essential act of faith of his life.

II *Rafael Alberti*

Like Gerardo Diego, Rafael Alberti was blessed with a natural talent for the poetic word, and like Lorca he was gifted with that magnetic personal quality the Andalusians call *gracia.* His initial books in the authentic neopopular manner (as Lorca's were not) confirmed both these qualities, but Alberti (like all the poets of this chapter) soon suffered a crisis of conscience which determined the direction of his life and poetry. He was the only one of his Generation to embrace and put into practice the political ideals of the Communist movement with a zeal at times detrimental to his poetry. But, while he has participated vigorously in the political atmosphere of his times, Alberti has unceasingly dedicated himself to the creation of his varied poetic work. Now secure in his reputation as a major poet, he has become the indomitable voice of the poet in permanent exile.

Rafael Alberti Merello, of Italian ancestry, was born near the Mediterranean port of Cadiz in 1902.[6] Since his family had fallen into straitened circumstances, the fact that he attended a Jesuit school as a charity student later determined his political leanings.

First attracted to painting, while living in the famous Residence of Students in Madrid along with Lorca, Dalí, Buñuel, and others, he soon shifted permanently to poetry. Toward 1928, he suffered a severe religious, political, and amorous crisis which stimulated his important book *Sobre los ángeles (Concerning the Angels)*. In 1930 he met and soon married María Teresa León, a beautiful young woman and a writer in her own right. The couple plunged into political activity during the years of the Republic and the Civil War. Escaping into exile after the war, Alberti found permanent refuge in Argentina. His postwar poetry usually concerns the rebuilding of his own life, a yearning for Spain and things lost, and an unceasing challenge against the oppressive rule there. In 1964 he took up residence in Rome, the home of his ancestors, and has continued his poetic activity.

Rafael Alberti achieved an instant reputation with the publication of *Marinero en tierra* (Sailor Ashore) in 1925.[7] Antonio Machado was a member of the jury which awarded it the National Prize; Jiménez immediately sent its author a letter of approbation. The obvious influences upon his first poetry, as Alberti later specified, were those of Gil Vicente, Jiménez himself, and above all the *Cancioneros*, books of anonymous traditional songs in short meters. The theme of *Sailor Ashore* is, as the title suggests, nostalgia for the sea — the sea as light, sound, rhythm, power, freedom.

> ¡ Quién cabalgara el caballo
> de espuma de la mar! . . .
> ¡ Amárrame a los cabellos,
> crin de los vientos de mar!
>   De un salto,
> quiero ganarme la mar.

> Oh, to bestride the horse
> Of the blue foam of the sea! . . .
> Fasten me by the hair,
> Mane of the winds of sea!
>   In a single bound
> I want to gain the sea.

The poet's epitaph is typical of the sailor's nostalgia for the sea:

> Si mi voz muriera en tierra,
> llevadla al nivel del mar
> y dejadla en la ribera.

> Should my voice die on land
> Take it down to the sea
> And leave it on the strand.

In a minor key *Sailor Ashore* approaches the theme of the return to the Andalusian paradise of Alberti's childhood. In *La amante* (The Beloved) Alberti continues in the neopopular manner, and his beloved wavers poetically between the sea and nostalgia, but his specific setting is the landscape of Old Castile around Burgos, Silos, and the River Duero — places consecrated by Machado. He rounds out this neopopular cycle with *El alba del alhelí,* which translates clumsily as *Dawn of the Gillyflower.*

Alberti's achievement in the neopopular manner is still considered important in his works. Having exhausted it for the moment, however, around 1927 he turned immediately to the two poetic currents swirling around him. This being the year of the tricentennial of Góngora, Alberti rapidly assimilated the complexities of Góngora's baroque form, as did Lorca and Diego, a form of rigid structure and metrics but of dazzling and ingenious metaphor. At the same time he seized upon the many experimental and irrational manners that were in the air, especially surrealism and futurism. The hybrid fruits of this experimentation are united in a single volume, *Cal y canto* (Lime and Stone), published in 1929. This title suggests the complexity of the poetry: *cal y canto* are the mason's materials, suggesting solidity of construction, but *canto* also means song in Spanish. Alberti demonstrates his virtuosity in the creation of tercets, *silvas,* and sonnets, the typical forms of Góngora. Naturally he includes a fragment of a *Soledad tercera* (Third Solitude), since Góngora left a first and a second. Perhaps the most impressive poems in this book are the impeccable neobaroque sonnets, among which "Amaranta" ("Amaranth") has become an anthology piece. This lady represents the fire and ice, have and have not, of the Renaissance:

> Rubios, pálidos senos de Amaranta,
> por una lengua de lebrel limados. . . .

> Blonde, smoothly polished breasts of Amaranth,
> Shaped by the slender greyhound's agile tongue. . . .

This potential fire is thwarted by a personified Solitude, who casts himself between Amaranth and the lover.

In 1928 Alberti suffered his crisis of conscience (which he called "love, wrath, rage, failure"), and he developed this upheaval in his important book *Sobre los ángeles (Concerning the Angels)*, published in 1929. Thus *Concerning the Angels* became the first book published in Spain under the influence of surrealism, those of Lorca, Aleixandre, and Cernuda appearing a bit later. For this reason perhaps, although the book seemed daring and shocking at the time, it is only vaguely and timidly surrealistic in expression. Certainly Alberti developed an original style of free verse, with short, fragmentary lines and modern imagery. And certainly he plunges into the depths of his consciousness in elaborating his spiritual and moral crisis.

Alberti's angels (which he seems to have discovered in Baudelaire) are modern in that they are opposing facets of his own consciousness, not separate protective entities. In his words, they are not "the Christian angels of the fine paintings and prints, but irresistible forces of the spirit, shaped to the most troubled and secret states of my nature."[8] In Alberti's angelology there are both good and bad angels, but his bad angels are legion, against which a single good angel must do battle.

The real problem in *Concerning the Angels* is the poet's crisis of identity, which he traces all the way back to his childhood and even beyond. The book begins with his crisis full upon him, with his "paradise lost" (title of the first poem). Both soul and hope are so utterly lost that he is searching for them in the nether world:

> Muerta en mí la esperanza,
> ese pórtico verde
> busco en las negras simas.

> With hope dead in me
> I seek that green portal
> in the dark abysses.

The poet is able to recover his paradise only fitfully through his "Three Remembrances of Heaven," which follow the "dreams" of the poet Bécquer. These remembrances take him back to that blissful state before time was, when love was an essence without body or name or sex — in his symbolic language, the sea was neither masculine nor feminine.

The prevailing mood of *Concerning the Angels*, typical of books in the surrealist manner, is one of rage, frustration, and despair, whose specific cause is a love betrayed. In this love the previously innocent poet's five senses have been awakened, especially that of touch associated with the body. In "El ángel de arena" ("Angel of Sand") he seems to confess that this was a forbidden love: "Vi que el mar verdadero era un muchacho que saltaba desnudo . . ." ("I saw that the real sea was a lad leaping nude . . ."). Therefore in "El ángel de carbón" ("Angel of coals") he reacts in horror. But ultimately there is a "good angel," the same one invoked by Antonio Machado, who comes at his desperate call and returns a "sweet light" to his breast, making his "soul navigable." And in the final poem, "El ángel superviviente" ("The Surviving Angel"), the one which survives is equal to the poet himself:

> La última voz de un hombre ensangrentó el viento.
> Todos los ángeles perdieron la vida.
> Menos uno, herido, alicortado.

> The final cry of a man bloodied the wind.
> All the angels lost their lives.
> Save one, wounded, with clipped wings.

He has emerged from this excruciating crisis a man, sadder, wiser, and imperfect like all human beings, but ready now to face the real world.

Shortly after this upheaval Alberti united with the companion of his life, the lady who (he declared later) rescued him from the "airless cave" in which he was agonizing and helped him return to the light. He then began to employ his poetic talents to attack the dead Establishment in Spain and to exalt the humble and the downtrodden, even becoming (in the ideal of our times) a "Poet in the Streets." However, during these years of political activity he found time and inspiration to write a moving and technically brilliant elegy upon the death of the bullfighter Ignacio Sánchez Mejías, in competition with that of Lorca. During the Civil War much of his poetry is circumstantial, but he succeeded in creating a number of enduring poems whose themes extol the heroic faith of the country lads turned soldiers in their unequal struggle against oppression.

After he settled in Córdoba, Argentina, in 1940, Alberti struggled successfully to regain the spiritual energy necessary to continue his work. His renascence is evident in his first volume published there, *Entre el clavel y la espada* (Between Carnation and Sword). Carnation and sword symbolize love and aggression or even life and death, and the powerful erotic imagery of this book emphasizes that the carnation prevails. Having written much loose poetry in the war years, Alberti seeks to recover "the precise word/ exact virgin verb with its proper adjective" in the demanding form of the sonnet. In the "Sonetos corporales" (Corporal Sonnets) the poet's vitality for life resurges in the form of sexual energy, a force "born in the thighs" that "smells of blood with lavender intermingled." A further real sign of the renewal of the life-force was the birth of Alberti's daughter Aitana in 1941, which provides the inspiration for his *Pleamar (High Tide)*. Her presence and promise as a "tender bough of sweet water" bring back in a flood the sea of Cádiz of his distant youth, and daughter, river, and sea ultimately become intermingled with the recovered rhythms of his poetry.

Alberti's later books of poetry reveal his multiple talents and continuing preoccupations. Always attracted to painting and painters, he moved outside his personal and political interests in his *A la pintura* (To Painting), succeeding beyond all expectations in capturing the color, line, and styles of painting in mere verbal structures. In his *Coplas de Juan Panadero* (Songs of Johnny Baker), modeled after Machado's *Juan de Mairena*, Alberti reaffirms his position as spokesman for the humble of the earth:

> Me llamo Juan Panadero,
> por la tierra y por el mar.
> El pan que amaso es de harina
> que nadie puede comprar.

> I'm simple Johnny Baker,
> On land and on the sea;
> My bread is from a grain
> No one can buy from me.

His *Retornos de lo vivo lejano* (Return to Living Memories; 1952) explores his bittersweet memories of Mother Spain and her "fierce sons" still separated by an "accursed shadow." Finally, his *Ora maritima*, which takes its title from an old Latin poem, is an homage to the trimillenium of Cádiz, his birthplace.

Although Alberti published a *Complete Poetry* in 1961, when he took up residence in Rome in 1964 the new experience provided the stimulus for his *Roma, peligro para caminantes* (Rome, Danger for Wayfarers). One of the impressive themes of this book is Alberti's development of the water symbols. Rome is of course the city of fountains, and the aging poet responds to the waters streaming sensuously over the nude statues, whereas all the cathedrals and towers and domes are to him dead monuments of a Christianity now alien to him. But it is in the simple act of "making water" that this still "salty" Andalusian finds his richest symbolism. In the sonnet "Se prohibe hacer aguas" (Making Water Forbidden), naturally everyone defies this bourgeois regulation and arches a merry stream. Even the aging poet himself responds to the stimulus, casts off his timidity and finds his own life force: "I lift my leg . . . I'm making water myself!" Finally he focuses this theme upon a carefree young man who has threatened to wet upon the old poet's very shoes. In his arching stream this young rascal symbolizes the freedom, naturalness, and defiance of bourgeois restrictions and hypocrisy that Alberti has envisioned for his own life.

Rafael Alberti has thus rounded off a career of intense dedication to the creation of a complete poetic works, while at the same time sustaining his political ideals. He has been the most consistent political rebel of his generation, although the domestic pattern of his mature life has been traditional. A poet of enormous natural talent, he has created a poetry characterized by variety. His achievement with various neopopular forms is impressive, from the simple song of his youth to the politically oriented *coplas* of his maturity. His *Concerning the Angels* in his modification of the surrealist manner is one of the essential books of intense personal crisis of his Generation. Generally a poet of form, he is a master of the sonnet. From the beginning cast by critics under the shadow of Lorca, he has carved out his own position through the power and originality of his mature work. Perhaps in his poetry Alberti fails somewhat to create a unified and original system, whereas Guillén and Aleixandre both succeeded, but his position seems secure as one of the major poets of the Generation of '27.

III *Vicente Aleixandre*

Along with Lorca and Guillén, Vicente Aleixandre has gradually become recognized as one of the three outstanding poets of his Generation for the original vision of the world expressed in his poetry and the distinct form of free verse in which he clothed it. As his major critic Carlos Bousoño has suggested, Aleixandre reached poetic maturity around 1930, a propitious time when the forces of irrationalism and individualism were at a peak in Spain.[9] Building upon the metaphysical freedom which Unamuno, Machado, and Jiménez had achieved at great cost, Aleixandre (like Lorca) rejected the historical and social world around him and created from his elemental passions a vast domain of cosmic and telluric forces anterior to man himself. Somewhat like Whitman, the poet moved grandly in the utter freedom of his own creation, above the historical strife going on around him. In his second period, the poet does an about-face and establishes intimate communication with man in his historical reality in the manner of most of the poets after the Civil War, but he has remained metaphysically uprooted upon the planet, emphasizing human brotherhood in the manner of Antonio Machado.

Although born in Seville in 1898, Vicente Aleixandre Merlo spent his childhood in the sun-drenched port of Málaga.[10] Moving to Madrid with his family in 1909, he studied law and commercial subjects, and began a career teaching commercial law while working at the same time for railway companies. In early maturity in 1925 he suffered a serious illness which forced his retirement; in 1932, after he had hit his stride as a poet, the illness returned and threatened his life itself. He then moved with the family of his parents to a home in the outskirts of Madrid where he has lived ever since. Thus Aleixandre's life has passed without change of scene and eventful details, in contrast to that of Lorca or Alberti. In 1949 he was inducted into the Royal Academy, and he has since become a revered figure for the poets of the younger generations, who have made his home a place of pilgrimage.

The poetry of Aleixandre falls clearly into two sharply defined periods. According to Aleixandre himself, his major theme in the first period is Creation itself, the solidarity of the elements of the cosmos. Through the impulse of primordial passion, the poet seeks to integrete himself totally with the cosmos. To achieve this unity, a kind of mystic pantheism, he must utilize the irrationalism and freedom available to him in order to escape the moral, psychological, and societal bonds which enchain him. Thus, surprisingly, man in his historical reality is absent in this phase of Aleixandre's poetry; there is only the poet and his passion, an intimate and at times frightening contact with the animal, vegetable, and mineral elements of the cosmos. The climax of this period comes when the poet achieves his "amorous solidarity" with creation through dissolution or "destruction" of his own identity. Such a pursuit implies a rebellion against his own culture, but Aleixandre (like Whitman) has generally preferred to operate beyond the level of culture rather than attack it directly. In his second period, beginning around 1945 and thus coinciding with the aftermath of the Civil

War, he continues his theme of "amorous solidarity," but now he
centers it directly in the historical reality of his *pueblo,* his "people."

A. *The First Period: Love as Freedom and Destruction*

Aleixandre's initial book, *Ambito* (Ambit), written during the
years 1924 - 27 under the influence of Jiménez, is typical of the first
efforts of his Generation. Then, around 1928, Aleixandre underwent
the tremendous crisis of conscience which provided the motive force
for his unique poetry. Interestingly, this crisis was generational
rather than individual, for Lorca, Alberti, and (a bit later) Cernuda
all suffered a comparable crisis critical for their poetry. Surely Aleixandre's crisis was triggered in part by the anxiety, frustration, and
rebellion which accompanied his crippling illness in early maturity.
Just at this time he discovered in the writings of Freud rich materials
applicable to his own psychic state — the power of the libido, the
effects of frustration, and the love-death conflict. Abandoning
abruptly the artistic forms and subtle themes of *Ambit,* Aleixandre
plunged into his subconscious and in rhythmic prose forms created
his first "difficult book," *Pasión de la Tierra* (Passion of the Earth).
Significantly, Aleixandre first called the book *Evasion toward the
Depths,* because the word "evasion" for the Generation of '27
usually suggests the normally prohibited, and in fact Aleixandre
found excuses not to publish the book until 1934, in Mexico.

Passion of the Earth is indeed a book of "dazzling obscurity," as
Gullón has said, but the general themes as a whole form a
meaningful pattern. In the general Freudian structure the poet's
outpouring of libido desperately seeks the love object, which
assumes multiple forms both attractive and repulsive, and the world
in total rises up to thwart his impulses, so that he constantly remains
threatened by a psychic death in his isolation. At the beginning the
poet declares his love, but the feminine figure is insufficient to contain it. At times the feminine figure is deformed, and therefore her
attraction is confusing.

> Me acuerdo que un día una sirena verde del
> color verde del color de la Luna sacó su pecho
> herido, partido en dos como una boca, y me
> quiso besar sobre la sombra muerta. . . .

> I remember that one day a green mermaid the
> color of the moon held out her wounded breast,
> parted in two like a mouth, and wanted me to
> kiss the dead shadow. . . .

This mermaid has only one breast, shaped like a mouth, which suggests the libido turning back upon itself. As Schwartz has analyzed it, Aleixandre's insistent breast symbolism suggests psychologically a return to the mother's breast, and hence a retreat from the anxieties and frustrations of the world.[11]

The fierce libidinal conflicts reach their most abysmal state in "La muerte o Antesala de Consulta" (Death or Waiting Room). In the doctor's waiting room the poet and the other "sick" wait in a deathlike anxiety. Although as lover he still protests his love, the beloved's kisses have "turned his stomach." Finally the first patient is called, but we do not know to what, since the waiting room itself is death. But toward the end of the book his usual dejection changes to a hope of triumph; through his love he wants to fuse with the sea, the sun, and finally light.

In 1929, Aleixandre was suddenly inspired to return to poetic form — a new form to be sure, of free verse with widely varying lines, staccato phrases and strange uses of connectors and relatives — but he continues to develop many of the themes of the first book in the Freudian-surrealist manner. This new volume bears the enigmatic title *Espadas como labios* (Swords like Lips). There is a powerful phallic thrust in the juxtaposition of the sword and the mouth; the phrase combines aggressive sexuality with his insistent buccal imagery. However, the fierce sexuality expected from this title never appears in this book (it explodes in Aleixandre's next one); in fact, the poet in his longing to be is so beset by anxieties that he tends to petrify reality.

As Dámaso Alonso has truly written, the poems of *Swords like Lips* do not have "common sense," but certain key ones indicate Aleixandre's progress in freeing his libidinal and poetic impulses once and for all.[12] In "Nacimiento último" (Ultimate Birth) his entire being is "on the alert" — "Alerta, alerta, alerta." It is worth noting that most of the poets of his Generation (Lorca, Guillén) use this word *alerta* each in his own way in poems which summarize an essential attitude toward life. Aleixandre's "ultimate birth" is that moment when he envisions the total freedom of his being:

> A mi paso he cantado porque he
>   dominado el horizonte . . .
> he visto el mar, la mar, los mares,
>   los no-límites.
> Soy alto como una juventud que no cesa.

Along my way I've sung because I've
                    dominated the horizon . . .
I've seen the masculine, the feminine sea,
            the seas, the no-limits.
I'm uplifted like youth that has no end.

In order to achieve this freedom of "no-limits, " the poet must reject the normal social and domestic traditions which are always present to ensnare him. In the brilliant poem "El vals" (The Waltz) he presents a caricature of the scene in the salon in which proper ladies and gentlemen whirl hypocritically toward matrimony. The waltz is of course the traditional, the passé, as jazz is the new and vital for this generation. As the dancers whirl, the ladies' "exuberant breasts on a tray" intensify the erotic attraction between the couples, until the unexpected climax is reached:

y ese beso que estaba (en el rincón) entre
                    dos bocas
se convertirá en una espina
que dispensará la muerte diciendo:
yo os amo.

and that kiss which was (in the corner) between
                    two mouths
will change into a thorn
which will dispense death saying:
I love you all.

Thus traditional domesticity, for which the poet feels both attraction and rejection, is a death for the free spirit.

Prostrated by his grave illness during the year 1932, Aleixandre gradually recovered the next year and in a sustained outburst of creative energy produced his first major book, *La destrucción o el amor* (Destruction or Love), which was promptly awarded the National Prize.[13] Undoubtedly dissatisfied with certain negative limitations of the Freudian-surrealist manner, Aleixandre merely assimilated this manner into an expanded vision which some have properly called neo-Romantic, for in his mystic pantheism the poet embraces the world itself in an all-consuming love. The new in Aleixandre is that he follows figures like Baudelaire in no longer viewing love as a fountain of life but as tragic destruction. His decision to embrace this tragic love is, as Bousoño alone has insisted, ethical, for in his modern conception there is absolutely no God, nor even an Oversoul. There is only the existential consciousness of the poet himself, fulfilling his tragic destiny through love as destruction. He utterly excludes the support and compassion of his fellow human beings, who are generally presented negatively, that is, they are dead to love. At times this love seems strangely Satanic, or suffused with hate; surprisingly, in this Aleixandre can be compared with Unamuno, despite the great differences between them.

After long reflection, Aleixandre himself has focused upon the theme of *Destruction or Love* and its importance in his work: "I believe that the poet's vision of the world achieves a first plenitude with this work, conceived under the central thought of the amorous unity of the universe."[14] The poet achieves a visionary transfiguration of the world in flux, a world at times luminous, at times foreboding, whose very essence is erotic love. Excluding spirit or any form of religious salvation, Aleixandre focuses upon matter itself, in the form of the human body, and in the erotic imagery of touch, kiss, and embrace. For him, perfect love can only be achieved in destroying himself and fusing with the cosmos. Thus fleeting human love is transformed through destruction into an enduring ecstasy of a strange dark mysticism. In his ambiguous title *Destruction or Love*, therefore, the conjunction *or* means "equal to," and this conjunction becomes a stylistic device with which he constantly equates dissimilar images and symbols.

The world of *Destruction or Love* is a vast domain in which the animal, vegetable, and mineral kingdoms are pulsating with primordial forces. The typical setting is the virgin jungle or the seashore, and especially in the jungle the poet is surrounded by a variety of wild animals, of which many are terrible and destructive in their natural pursuits, some innocent and helpless. This is also a world of great natural elements, such as sea and river, mountains and plain, sky and stars. And in this universe, there is constant interaction between the poet and the specific body of the beloved and all the other forces. In this primordial erotic tension, the body is constantly being transformed into river or sea or sky or mountain, and conversely the natural elements assume human qualities in their natural attraction and destruction.

The book clearly begins in a mood of aggression barely controlled, where

> tigres del tamaño del odio,
> leones como un corazón hirsuto,

> sangre como la tristeza aplacada,
> se baten como la hiena amarilla. . . .

> tigers the size of hate,
> lions like a hairy heart,
> blood like placated sadness,
> clash together like the yellow hyena. . . .

In this poem, "La selva y el mar" (Jungle and Sea), the poet continues by introducing a series of aggressive animals to which he later dedicates individual poems: the tiger, the hunting lion, the elephant with his tusks, the cobra "which resembles the most burning love," and even the tiny scorpion, who with its pincers seizes "an instant of life." Of course, the poet identifies with these animals, both the magnificent and the humble. In "Cobra" this animal of "most burning love" is phallic (and thus erotic) in its very shape, and in its fanged strike becomes the perfect instrument of destruction — which for Aleixandre is of course love. Finally even the humble beetle merits its "word" in "El escarabajo." This diminutive being enclosed in its dark shell accepts the reality that it is no butterfy, but it, too, is a living thing, capable of "the dark memory of love." This particular group of poems, scattered throughout the book, forms a powerful nucleus in *Destruction or Love*.

Early in the book Aleixandre projects his total theme in the much-anthologized poem "Unity in Her" ("Unidad en ella"). His primary impulse bursts forth from his contact with the human body:

> Cuerpo feliz que fluye entre mis manos,
> rostro amado donde contemplo el mundo,
> donde graciosos pájaros se copian fugitivos,
> volando a la región donde nada se olvida.

> Joyful body which flows between my hands,
> beloved face where I contemplate the world,
> where graceful birds fugitively copy one another
> flying off to the region where nothing is forgotten.

The fiercely erotic pursuit of this "body" leads the poet inevitably onward toward that final possession in which love and death are one:

> Quiero amor o la muerte, quiero morir del todo,
> quiero ser tú, tu sangre, esa lava rugiente

> que regando encerrada bellos miembros extremos
> siente así los hermosos límites de la vida.

> I want love or death, I want to die utterly,
> I want to be you, your blood, that raging lava
> which enclosed, irrigating lovely extremities,
> feels thus the beautiful limits of life.

In this "unity in her," Aleixandre with the generic pronoun emphasizes the shifting and expanding meanings of the Feminine. Essentially the Feminine includes all the seductive forms of Nature herself — never a real woman; and the final seductive form is Death, always feminine in Spanish. He objectifies his theme even further in the final lines of this poem. This kiss of love, like a "slow thorn," is a "vengeful light, light or mortal sword" suspended menacingly above his neck, but it "can never destroy the unity of this world."

Despite the many expressions of incurable solitude, veiled aggression, and threatening despair, the poet moves firmly toward the triumph of love, the specific theme of many poems, among which Aleixandre himself preferred "Se querían" (They Loved Each Other). But perhaps even more moving and personal is the poem entitled "Triunfo de amor" (Triumph of Love). Love comes first under the moon, an entity for Aleixandre seductive, ambivalent, tragic, even malevolent; but triumphant and enduring love bursts forth under the light of the sun.

> El puro corazón adorado, la verdad de la vida,
> la certeza presente de un amor irradiante,
> su luz sobre los ríos, su desnudo mojado,
> todo vive, pervive, sobrevive y asciende
> como un ascua luciente de deseo en los cielos.

> The pure heart adored, the truth of life,
> the present certainty of a radiant love,
> its light above the rivers, its nude dripping water,
> everything lives, persists, survives and ascends
> like a lucent coal of desire toward the heavens.

Naturally *Destruction or Love* ends in death, the title ("Muerte") of the final poem, and death at the last is not that triumphant consummation when it is fused with love. Death is that "eternal name without date," a "sea of impious lead," "that tunnel where color is dissolved." Death is finally a number of little things:

> Muerte como un puñado de arena,
> como el agua que en el hoyo queda solitaria,
> como la gaviota que en medio de la noche
> tiene un color de sangre sobre el mar que no existe.

> Death like a fistful of sand,
> like solitary water that in a hole remains,
> like a seagull that in the lovely night
> has the color of blood on a non-existent sea.

After the expense of passion in *Destruction or Love,* Aleixandre predictably falls into a deep depression of spirit, and during the years 1934 - 36 he surrendered to this depression in the creation of his most pessimistic book, *Mundo a solas* (World Alone), not published until 1950. Finally recovering from the depths but still unwilling to face the world of man in his historical reality, Aleixandre refocused his vision of the amorous solidarity of the cosmos in his next great book, *Sombra del paraíso* (Shadow of Paradise), written between 1939 - 43, in the desolate aftermath of the Civil War. Like Cernuda, Aleixandre returns to the Andalusian paradise of his childhood, the state of pristine innocence anterior to sin and suffering, when the light and sky of Málaga and the Mediterranean were perfection itself. Moreover, by extension this Andalusian paradise becomes a vision of the universe at the dawn of creation, before the appearance of man himself and his tragic strife. In such a world Aleixandre almost abandons the veiled agression and threatening negativism of *Destruction or Love;* but, significantly, in the limiting *Shadow* of his title he acknowledges that modern man cannot even envision a pure paradise. In fact. although many powerful poems reiterate his theme of cosmic solidarity, this paradise is ultimately threatened by the poet's existential loneliness, by his painful existence in time and memory.

In the opening poem, "Criaturas de la aurora" ("Creatures of the Dawn"), his vision is one of the perfect harmony of things, even before the appearance of the word. All creatures enjoyed the "generous light of innocence"; the birds were born anew each morning, birds of "initial happiness," still capable of flight though bathed in the sensuous dew. Pleasure still did not have the "fearful name" of pleasure. But this lucent vision is tinged with melancholy by the fact that all the poet's verbs are in the past tense.

In this world of dawn the poet next evokes the particular world of his childhood. In memory his river (the Guadalhorca) flowed so gently that it seemed not to flow; in fact it seemed "miraculous dew" that the child could contain in his hand, not a symbol of life passing. His "city of paradise" (Málaga), which hangs almost suspended from the mountains overlooking the bay, was a magic place which "flew with open wings" in the translucent atmosphere of the seashore. His sea (the Mediterranean) he approaches from present time, with the "dust of the earth upon his shoulders," but the sea itself is a symbol for his amorous solidarity:

> . . . heme aquí, luz eterna,
> vasto mar sin cansancio,
> última expresión de un amor que no acaba,
> rosa del mundo ardiente.

> . . . behold me here, eternal light,
> vast sea without weariness,
> ultimate expression of a love that has no end,
> rose of the burning world.

Still sustained by his amorous vision, Aleixandre repeats the theme (though of course not the form of expression) of his earlier poems. In another "Plenitude of Love" he lovingly recreates the "dripping nude" of the beloved, the ultimate matter of the earth.

> ¡Ah, maravilla lúcida de tu cuerpo cantado,
> destellando de besos sobre tu piel despierta;
> bóveda centelleante nocturnamente hermosa,
> que humedece mi pecho de estrellas o de espumas!

> Oh, lucid marvel of your body singing,
> flashing kisses upon your awakened flesh;
> sparkling firmament nocturnally beautiful,
> that moistens my breast with seafoam or with stars!

But under the temporal pressures of his existence the shadows upon his paradise lengthen and threaten to engulf it. In "Padre mío" (My Father) the poet evokes the memory of his real father when the poet was a child and the world was intact. Clearly the death of the father was a first sign of mortality. In the final poem, "No basta" (Not Enough) the death of the father has perhaps prefigured the death of God Himself. The light of the sun (common symbol of the father), the beloved's look, even the seas are "not enough," the poet starkly intones, and he falls into a total despair.

> Sobre la tierra mi bulto cayó. Los cielos eran
> sólo conciencia mía, soledad absoluta.
> Un vacío de Dios sentí sobre mi carne . . .
> y besé sólo a la tierra, a la oscura, sola,
> desesperada tierra que me acogía.

> Upon the earth my bulk fell. The heavens were
> only my own consciousness, absolute solitude.
> An emptiness of God I felt upon my flesh . . .
> and I kissed only the earth, the dark, solitary,
> despairing earth which gave me refuge.

These simple lines are a reasonable expression of the existential metaphysics of our times. Although Aleixandre, like all of his Generation except Diego, stubbornly formulated his metaphysics upon this earth and the persistence of matter alone, his awareness of the "emptiness of God" emphasizes his kinship with Unamuno in his hunger for a personal God. Having lost the Father, he turns pitifully to the mother, to the mother's lap of his childhood, for now even the world is "not enough." It is not surprising that he ultimately begins that return, typical of modern man, to suffering humanity itself. His "Hijos de los campos" (Sons of the Soil) prefigures the essential theme found throughout the second period of his poetry.

These two great books *Destruction or Love* and *Shadow of Paradise* form the cornerstones of Aleixandre's poetry.[15] In them he develops with astonishing completeness and originality his metaphysical vision of the amorous solidarity of the cosmos, a tragic vision, to be sure. In them he demonstrates a mastery of free verse unparalleled in Spanish poetry. And in them he develops a poetic technique with symbol, image, and metaphor which Bousoño has convincingly declared is original, although other poets of this Generation participated in this renovation. His development of the visionary image, which involves the imaginative free association of surrealism, and of the extended symbol are quite impressive. His creation of an original syntax involves the use of the conjunction *or* to achieve a type of simile, and the use of negatives to express a positive sense — a technique adapted from Góngora. With this achievement locked up permanently in these books, Aleixandre turns to another poetic task more typical of our times.

B. *The Poet in Time and History*

It is perhaps with a feeling of relief that the reader turns from the difficult and turbulent world of Aleixandre's first period with its cosmic and telluric dimensions to the quieter and simpler but no less moving world of his second phase. By 1945 Aleixandre has sensed the prevailing current of the times, and in Spain he in fact helps to lead the new direction. He soon discovers that (in our contemporary parlance) "poetry is communication," and his major theme becomes human solidarity, with compassion toward all human beings living in time. His first book in the new manner is *Historia del corazón* (History of the Heart), written during the years 1945 - 53. "History" for this generation means the direct experience of the poet and his fellow human beings, both in the past and the present; "the heart" is of course the collective heart, the joys and pains of all.

History of the Heart begins with Aleixandre's typical preoccupation with his own love, whose basic quality is now its ephemerality. Love is "like the thistledown" ("Como el cardo"), for even in the beloved's arms,

> el amante sabe que pasa,
> que el amor mismo pasa,
> y que este fuego generoso que en él no pasa,
> presencia puro el tránsito dulcísimo
>   de lo que eternamente pasa.

> the lover knows that it passes,
> that love itself passes,
> and that this generous fire which in him passes not,
> witnesses pure the sweet passage of
>   that which eternally passes.

Through this "generous fire" enkindled in him the poet is able to reach out to others, especially those who have not had the fortune to love. But first he must record the death of his own personal love. In "Nombre" (Name) he tries for twenty-eight lines to say aloud the beloved's name — yet he cannot or will not; there is always in Aleixandre an ambiguity, a holding back, a something not said. And in "El último amor" (The Last Love) his love reaches annihilation, this time without transformations.

The poet can then in his "extended look" reach out to the world outside his own heart. He goes out to the town square, source of Spanish life, and mingles with the people enjoying the friendly sun.

He visits a humble home, where the father, mother, and children are performing the simple tasks of living. He focuses upon an old man, wrinkled with age but patient and resigned, who is enjoying the light and warmth of the sun. In fact he becomes a "vagabond," by which he indicates he is always an outsider, reaching out in compassion but never quite participating, never quite living with his humanity.

As is typical in Aleixandre, *History of the Heart* ends in a form of death. As he summarizes existence, "Entre dos oscuridades, un relámpago"; that is, between the obscurity of birth and that of death life is a lightning flash. Although "we eat shadow," man in his nobility should with sadness and tenderness accept what is to come. Life is its own consolation, and consciousness somehow continues to exist.

In his last great book *En un vasto dominio* (In a Vast Dominion), written between 1958 and 1962, Aleixandre amplifies the theme of human solidarity with consistent objectivity. This "vast dominion," not the cosmos of before, is man of flesh and blood and limb in the historical and living reality which surrounds him. In structure, the book is a series of "incorporations," which begin with human matter itself, from which the human organs are developed. Moreover, each section is a "chapter," a word which suggests the novel, in which human experience is narrated. In complete maturity, Aleixandre attempts the difficult task of beginning with human matter and tracing the development of the specific organs which make man a functional being — trunk, leg, arm, hand, head, eye, ear, mouth, even the eyelashes. Then, having created this man before our eyes, the poet moves outward to the surrounding world, a Spanish world finally; and, in the manner of Unamuno perhaps, he dwells with moving compassion upon the timeless Spanish village with its white-walled cemetery, its deserted square, and its humble inhabitants. He focuses toward the past upon towns with a rich history, now struggling humbly to survive. In addition to the young mother, his most adequate symbol for the continuity of life is the couple. In a simple scene the young couple, secure for the moment in their love and laughter, are presented at their window, looking out upon the life around them. This couple through love achieves the continuity of matter, for Aleixandre the ultimate reality. In his final poem he summarizes this concept: "Everything is matter: time,/ Space; flesh and work." For Aleixandre, only matter endures, matter which is both flesh and spirit in one; matter whose most perfect form is the "dew-kissed nude" of his earlier period and the human body of the infant, the mother, the old man in his final years.

Perhaps a significant addition to this record is the poem with which Aleixandre closes his *Complete Poetry*. On the occasion of the death of André Bretón, the father of surrealism, Aleixandre remembers by association Lorca's *Poet in New York*, Cernuda's *A River, a Love*, Alberti's *Concerning the Angels*, and his own *Destruction or Love*. Thus these four poets, all Andalusians, are for Aleixandre fallen angels, tragic rebels, all seeking "light or destruction"; that is, in his tragic philosophy light equals destruction.

Aleixandre's final book (or so the title suggests), published at seventy, and forty years after his initial *Ambit*, is *Poemas de la consumación* (Poems of Consummation).[16] The final consummation is of course death, and for this ultimate reality the poet has gone back inside himself. For him, youth (and thus the capacity for love) is synonymous with life; therefore, the old man merely exists in an "opaque crystal," already separated from life. But, in poems of utter simplicity, he accepts this final state without tears or sighs or pleas for mercy.

Vicente Aleixandre is one of the most original Spanish poets of this century. In his poetry of two major periods he created an original and coherent vision of the universe based upon the amorous solidarity of humanity. Rejecting (or going beyond) the culture around him, he sought a perfect fusion with the elements of nature, expressed with the images of erotic love. Through this fusion, love becomes destruction, destruction becomes death as the final liberation. In his second period, he attempted to break out of his cosmic isolation and to approach mankind directly, still rejecting culture. As any great poet must, he expressed his vision in an original style of surrealist, Freudian, and neo-Romantic elements. He is the acknowledged master of free verse in Spain, surpassing both Jiménez and Lorca. His development of the visionary image and symbol, a technique also used by Lorca and Cernuda, added a new dimension to Spanish poetry. Aleixandre's poetry is extremely difficult (even hermetic) in his first period, surprisingly clear and simple in expression in his second; both manners have been deemed fitting for our complex times. Like Jiménez and Guillén, Aleixandre offers an extensive and complete metaphysical structure in his poetry, in which all the parts combine and complement each other. With his poetry and his presence, he has exerted a major influence upon the Spanish poets since 1939.

IV   *Luis Cernuda*

It was only in the decade of the sixties that Luis Cernuda finally achieved recognition as one of the major poets of the Generation of '27. Following the publication in 1958 of the third edition of his collected poems *La realidad y el deseo* (Reality and Desire) in Mexico, his poetry of alienation and self-assertion touched a responsive chord in the agitated sixties. Always considered the "baby" of his group by his peers (despite his nearness to them in age), Cernuda proved to be the most complete rebel of his generation, in theme, form, and life style. From his embattled position, this gentle soul infuriated almost everyone, even the Master Jiménez, but his poetry projects an impressive sincerity of conviction and a lifetime dedication to the art and craft of poetry.

Born in Seville in 1902, Cernuda (like Jiménez, Lorca, and Alberti) was thus from Andalusia, that particular Andalusia of brilliant Mediterranean light, blue skies, whitewashed walls, and multicolored flowers. A melancholy and introspective child, he discovered the poetic world through the Sevillian Bécquer and received encouragement in the university from the poet Pedro Salinas, then a professor there. He published his first book of poetry, *Perfil del aire* (Profile of the Air), in 1927; the fact that reviews of it were negative or lukewarm disconcerted and alienated the easily wounded poet permanently. Like Lorca he discovered no attractive profession, but the realities of life forced him into a permanent role as lecturer and professor of Spanish literature. He began his wandering professorship in France, then returned to Madrid. In 1938, escaping from war-torn Madrid, Cernuda wound up in the hated industrial city of Glasgow, later transferring to London, where he learned to respect (even if he could not like) the English. After World War II he came to Mount Holyoke College and spent some relatively peaceful years; in 1952 he abandoned this secure position and took up residence in Mexico, to be near an autumn love and to be in an Hispanic atmosphere. Fulfilling his own premonitions, he died of a heart attack in 1963, only sixty-one years old.

As early as 1936 Cernuda formulated his philosophy of life and poetry under the title *Reality and Desire*, and ultimately the eleven separate collections of his poems were organized under this title. His book is therefore his spiritual autobiography, and his constant struggle was to transmute his intense personal experience into an objective poem. Given his talent as a critic, Cernuda himself focused upon the conflict between reality and desire: "I was drawn by desire towards the reality that lay before my eyes as if it were only by its possession that I could become convinced that I existed."[17] As an adolescent, perhaps he briefly enjoyed the fusion of desire and reality in communion with nature. As he recorded it later in a poem, a "fair angel" helped him to total awareness of "some dense golden-yellow tulips/ Lifted up in joy among green swords," tulips which symbolized the beauty and oneness of life. Ideally, for him "the secret essence of poetry . . . resides in the conflict between reality and desire, between appearance and truth, which permits us to gain a glimpse of that complete picture of the world of which we are unaware."[18]

In late adolescence, Cernuda enjoyed for a brief moment that complete picture of the world in an intense vision of love for an Andalusian lad by the seashore.[19] This vision of love, somewhat like Shakespeare's perhaps, immediately crashed against Cernuda's own ethical and religious background, and his traditional Spanish culture. Reality became the hostile world around him, especially the world of people and normal customs, and he retreated with his desire into a paradise, adopting Virgil's famous phrase "Et in Arcadia ego." This paradise is Arcadian and not Edenic for the subtle reason of excluding Eve. In his ensuing battle with reality, Cernuda fortified himself with André Gide's positive defense of homosexuality, and he began a long struggle to assert the right to his desires as being essential to his very identity. At first he retreated into a bitter evasion in his poetry; then when he dared to project his desires openly he had to bear the concealed and sometimes hypocritical disapproval of some of his fellow poets and the critics. As Cernuda matured as a poet his homosexuality became a symbol for man's alienation in society, and indeed for his ontological solitude in the universe.

Cernuda's first book of poetry, *Profile of the Air*, which he later modestly changed to *Primeras poesías* (First Poems), reveals much of the impressionistic manner of Juan Ramón Jiménez and a bit of the direction he is shortly to follow. In this book he emphasizes his symbol of the garden, his Arcadian paradise surrounded by walls which shut out the real world. Cernuda continues the theme of the poet in the solitude of an idealized world in *Egloga, elegía, oda* (Eclogue, Elegy, Ode), a title which suggests his return to Renaissance forms and manner. Early in life Cernuda developed an enduring admiration for Garcilaso de la Vega, prototype of the Renaissance ideal, whose melancholy eclogues provide no hint of his soldierly life. While these poems are thus imitative, in the "Ode"

Cernuda clearly establishes his own dominant theme. Whereas in Garcilaso chaste nymphs ripple the crystalline waters, in Cernuda a golden youth, a young "god," "Perfect body in the vigor of youth," cavorts in his hidden crystalline pool, existing entirely within his own sensuality.

After these initial efforts, whose artificial beauty disgusted even their creator, Cernuda in 1929 made a complete change of direction and embraced the poetic variation of the surrealistic mode then winning adherents in Spain. In his *Un río, un amor* (A River, a Love), the positive title belies the actual content of the book. The protagonist in fact endures in a limbo of bodies in agony, sad winds, complete darkness, red seas, tears, closed doors, "assassinated birds," and thus absolute alienation. In angry dejection the poet in two of his essential lines summarizes his philosophy of love: "Fury color of love,/ Love color of oblivion." Throughout the book he is enduring in a state of oblivion, exhausting his imagery in projecting its negative qualities.

Beginning with *A River, a Love*, Cernuda employs what Bousoño has called (in connection with Aleixandre) the "visionary image," a free association twice removed from reality. In a striking poem, he seeks to convey the feeling that his former poetic indolence has become "tiredness" of both body and soul:

> Estar cansado tiene plumas,
> Tiene plumas graciosas como un loro,
> Plumas que desde luego nunca vuelan
> Mas balbucean igual que un loro.

> Being tired has feathers
> Has graceful feathers like a parrot,
> Feathers that after all never fly,
> But babble just like the parrot.

The parrot is here a negative symbol of the color, movement, and sounds of the natural world, since it cannot fly and its "babble" is useless. The theme of the poem therefore becomes the poet's uselessness and world-weariness.[20]

In *Los placeres prohibidos* (Forbidden Pleasures; 1931), Cernuda comes closer to breaking out of the prison of his frustrations, and he declares himself ready to challenge the restrictions of society. From the beginning he realizes that his personal desires involve an ethical decision:

Diré cómo nacisteis, placeres prohibidos,
Como nace un deseo sobre torres de espanto. . . .

I'll say how you were born, forbidden pleasures,
As a desire is born upon towers of fear. . . .

These "towers of fear," the consciousness of good and evil instilled in the poet by training, must be cast down, and he, like Walt Whitman, exalts total liberty, the "liberty of love." By now the poet has resolved to liberate himself from the restrictions of society, but he in fact has no love, only the memory of his youth and the "unending dream" of the future.

During this turbulent period Cernuda suffered a brief but ugly love affair in Madrid, which pushed him down to the lowest point in his life. In rereading Bécquer, he discovered the Romantic poet's awareness of the dark void, and one of Bécquer's phrases became the title of the final book in this period of his poetry: *Donde habite el olvido* (Where Oblivion Dwells). Returning to a lyrical form vaguely reminiscent of Bécquer's, the poet contrasts the innocence and plenitude of the Arcadian dreams of his youth with the desolation of his present situation. In the bloom of youth, his days were "identical to clouds"; now, in phrases reminiscent of Lorca, the structure of his life and even his poetry are threatened: "Earth, earth and desire. A form lost."

In the utter desolation of this psychological impasse, Luis Cernuda came to terms with himself and with life. He accepted alienation as the basic human condition, the theme developed in his poem "The Soliloquy of the Lighthouse Keeper." He now understood that this isolation was in fact the liberty he had fought for valiantly, the freedom existential man must assume in order to forge his own identity. And he discovered in the German poet Hölderlin a renewed dedication to poetry, not as a personal unburdening, but as construction and craft and thematic development. His "Hymn to Sadness" reveals this new direction in both form and theme; hereafter his typical poem is elegiac in tone.

In *Las nubes* (The Clouds), which spans the years 1937 - 1940, Cernuda in his new elegiac manner records his reaction to the Spanish Civil War and his growing spiritual preoccupations in his early years of exile. In "To a Poet Dead," he laments the fact that the blindly reactionary elements in Spanish society have destroyed a poet like Lorca, who represents vitality and promise. His "Spanish Elegy" mourns the loss of the spiritual greatness of Mother Spain;

Cernuda no less than Unamuno and Machado retained a stubborn dream of a revitalized Spain. Later, in Glasgow, Cernuda projected the death of his dream in the symbolic figure of an exile who spoke with him, then disappeared into the night, saying "Spain has died." In his solitude in Glasgow his pressing spiritual concerns are evidenced in poems such as "The Visit of God." God comes because of the poet's need, but the poet is so urgent with skeptical questions that he hardly waits for a reply. In "Lazarus," Cernuda creates a *persona* from this biblical character to project his own painful rebirth after the Civil War. Lazarus describes his terrible struggle to be reborn, only to find that he is reborn aged in both body and spirit. He is impressed only by the beauty of Jesus' face, and his only lesson learned is that "beauty is patience."

In his two later major collections *Como quien espera el alba* (Awaiting the Dawn; 1944) and *Con las horas contadas* (With Time Running Out; 1956), Cernuda continues to create effective poems of varied theme. In "The Family," addressing himself in the second person for distance, the poet recalls his "stern father, scatterbrained mother, impossible older sister"; his point is that he has cut all ties with family, and deliberately lives spiritually alone. His "Apologia pro vita sua" attempts to justify his life before both mankind and God; his only regret is the sins that he did not have "the occasion or the strength to commit." Over against these typical poems of rebellion and alienation, Cernuda continues to produce pure lyrics such as "The Hawthorns," in which the poet reaffirms that his only salvation is to contemplate in the present the beauty of the hawthorns bursting into white and purple bloom.

Surely after serious thought Cernuda placed at the end of *Reality and Desire* a strange poem with the English title "Birds in the Night" which summarizes his love-hate relation with the world. The poem records that French (or English) officialdom has placed a plaque at 8 Great College Street in London to commemorate the fact that Verlaine and Rimbaud once lived there for a few months. What is not mentioned, Cernuda notes, is that the "odd couple" actually spent a tormented honeymoon in the house. Verlaine was the prototype of the delicate lyric poet, Rimbaud the rebellious genius. Both later lived through various sordid episodes which scandalized their society. Now all this is obscured, and officialdom uses them even as a tourist attraction. In literary circles Verlaine is out of fashion, Rimbaud a god of the critics. For Cernuda, both truly "lived and died for the word," that is, for poetry. Rimbaud himself, says Cernuda, once wished that humanity had one head, so he could cut it off. No, insists Cernuda, would that humanity were a single cockroach so that he could smash it underfoot.

Luis Cernuda, despite his gentle and delicate nature, is perhaps the fiercest rebel in a rebellious century in Spain. In his youth his "desire" created an Arcadian myth in which beautiful lads enjoyed a paradise of the senses; reality intruded in the form of a hostile world. But the poet never retreated, and his struggle for his own vital expression became a struggle to establish his identity in keeping with his dream. His Spanish culture reacted predictably against him, though perhaps not as implacably as he imagined, but he dedicated his life to an attempt to establish his "dignity." He called his book *Reality and Desire*, and in it he oscillated between flagellation of the hostile world around him and the creation of his own identity according to his desire, mainly of the love of beauty. As he matured, he succeeded in objectifying his personal desires in solid poems with the stamp of his own style. Although he remained in alienation from his countrymen and even humanity itself, such is the sincerity of his spiritual autobiography that his Hispanic culture has already taken the wayward son back into the fold.

CHAPTER 8

Spanish Poetry Since 1939

FOLLOWING the plan chosen for this book, we have dedicated our essential but limited space to the major Spanish poets of the twentieth century whose work is now complete, or substantially so, and whose reputations have been established with some measure of permanence. Naturally the traditions continued and developed by these great poets have been passed on to the succeeding generations, and since 1939 an impressive group of fine poets has arisen to carry on generally in the tradition of Unamuno and Machado, with specific influence of their themes as reflected in Aleixandre and Dámaso Alonso of the Generation of '27.[1] Unamuno's major themes concern man in his direct experience (even domestic experience), his struggle for a living God and his love-hate relation with his troubled Spain. Machado, who pursued all three of these themes, gradually emphasized yet another: that of man in his temporal and social situation, the theme of brotherhood. Clearly Machado's general influence has gradually permeated the post-Civil War period, for the major theme since 1939 has been man in his historical and social reality, man situated in irreversible time and localized in space.

The essential difference between the Generations of 1898 and 1927 and the post-Civil War poets involves the belief in poetry itself. For Jiménez and Machado, for Guillén, Lorca, and Aleixandre, the creation of poetry was ultimately an act of faith, in a sense their only faith. The extreme example of Jiménez is instructive. As a symbolist, Jiménez believed in the efficacy of the symbol and the semidivine powers of the poet in utilizing it to reveal transcendence. Under the pressures of the progressive disintegration exemplified by the Civil War and its aftermath, this faith in poets and poetry has eroded, and the poets since 1939 have declared themselves humble figures, struggling equally with their brothers in humanity. Predictably the

139

influence of Jiménez has faded, and Machado, who believed in poetry but who believed more intensely in the brotherhood of man, became the prophet of the new generations.

By common consent the poet of transition between the two periods is Miguel Hernández, a tragic figure who seems like a younger brother of Lorca.[2] Developing in the years just before the Civil War, Hernández, while serving as a soldier, continued to create his poetry of life and love threatened by destruction, and he died in prison at thirty-two in the aftermath. In his youth Hernández was briefly a shepherd of flocks, so that a bit of the popular myth of the unlettered natural poet has enhanced his reputation. Actually when he came to Madrid he rapidly assimilated the literary currents around him, especially the cultured stream associated with the revival of Góngora, characterized by difficult metaphor and polished technical forms. Hernández demonstrated his mastery of this manner in his first major book, *El rayo que no cesa* (The Flash that Never Ceases). In the tradition of Lorca and Aleixandre, this personal book develops the theme of the painful awakening of love in the poet. This tragic love is integrated into what he correctly foresees as his destiny of pain and death. In perhaps the central sonnet of the book he concentrates his own destiny in the symbol of the Spanish fighting bull. Like the dark bull, he is a creature of power and passion, but he is also "born for mourning and for pain," born for the destiny of the sword of death. Even in this book he seeks to escape his tragic solitude by turning to the nameless peasants of his origins and their humble but communal life.

With the outbreak of the war Hernández abandons his personal solitude and difficult forms and returns to the people, their cause, and the popular forms of expression. Previously, he was pursuing culture; now he becomes "clay," the living substance of the earth, in order to struggle against the threatening destruction of life itself. In *Viento del pueblo* (Wind of the People) and *El hombre acecha* (Man in Ambush), he becomes the voice of his people in the manner of Alberti and the Chilean poet Pablo Neruda. Accepting the destruction of his own generation, the poet becomes the soldier-husband who focuses fiercely upon the womb of woman, for the son born of this union is the only hope for the future. As Hernández foresaw, it was his fate to live the tragedy of the Civil War, but he emerged from it as a man and poet touched by myth, and thus a symbol for the succeeding generations.

Immediately after the war, in which of course the reactionary forces prevailed, the first signs of a rebirth of poetry are associated with the appearance of the literary journal *Garcilaso*. Led by José García Nieto, the poets of this brief movement attempted to retreat into the safety of a poetry vaguely like Garcilaso's. This Renaissance poet naturally sang in the Petrarchan manner his melancholy lyrics of Neoplatonic love in the traditional forms of the sonnet and the *silva*. In this way the poets could expend their energies in the safety of sonorous rhymes and well-turned phrases, without offending anyone. Of course this movement endured only until the revolutionary voices typical of modern times recovered their impetus and direction.

The year 1944 is a key date in the development of postwar poetry in Spain. In that year, Dámaso Alonso, by all rights the major critic of the Generation of '27 but also for many one of its major poets,[3] published his *Hijos de la ira* (Children of Wrath).[4] This title admirably sums up the postwar feeling of rage, guilt, and spiritual frustration. His first line in both its prosaic form and exaggerated idea recapitulates the theme: "Madrid is a city of more than one million corpses (according to the latest statistics)." Assuming a prophetic tone, the poet does not blame outside forces for the death and destruction upon the land; in his sackcloth and ashes he excoriates himself. In typical Old Testament imagery he wallows in pestilence and putrefaction and casts himself in evil taverns and houses of prostitution. But in concentrating guilt upon himself, by extension he accuses all of mankind. In an existential torment reminiscent of Unamuno, the poet ultimately centers his struggle upon the God lost to himself and his people and attempts to invoke His presence, terrible though it may be. Although the God of love never reveals His presence, the possibility of love exists upon this earth. The poet progresses from a "thing," perhaps a stone, to the tree, which represents pantheistic love; finally he discovers a redeeming love in the figure of woman, in the mother, and in the Virgin. This possible salvation by the feminine is summed up perhaps in "Mujer con alcuza" (Woman with Cruet), in which the lady is Spain herself. Thus in this book of a certain biblical grandiloquence Dámaso Alonso provides a kind of catharsis for himself and the Spanish people. Moreover, the original free verse in which it is written, alternating between rolling periods and the colloquial rhythms of speech, with common and even vulgar vocabulary, with tremendous images and metaphors, becomes a source book for later poets.

Another literary event of importance in 1944 was the publication of Vicente Aleixandre's *Shadow of Paradise*. Although in this book Aleixandre retains much of the "cosmic" manner of his first period in his quest for a lost paradise, already he is making the transition to a poetry of direct human emotion. In his poems for the city of Málaga, for his father now dead, and for the humble tillers of the soil, he expresses in simple free verse human emotions which struck a responsive chord. Moreover, according to the direct testimony of later poets, his physical presence as a poet already revered and eager to offer encouragement proved to be a powerful stimulus for the developing postwar poets. After he finally published *History of the Heart* in 1954, Aleixandre's influence continued to grow and has continued almost to the present day.

From 1945 until around 1963 there developed a significant group of poets generally dedicated to the theme of man in his temporal and social reality. In their temporal concerns these poets approach life as direct experience in the here and now; life is a *quehacer*, a thing to do, to be expressed in narrative form. In their social concerns, while some are more revolutionary than others, all are preoccupied with social injustices and the sufferings and desires of the common man. In form these poets often employ a free verse of colloquial tone and simple metaphor; even when they use traditional forms, it is obvious that they are directing themselves to the average reader. In fact, the worst sin is to write down to the reader, who is considered a brother and equal to the poet, and the aesthete is directly scorned. Among the outstanding poets of this period can be included José Luis Hidalgo, Vicente Gaos, Luis Rosales, Leopoldo Panero, José Hierro, Luis Felipe Vivanco, Angela Figuera, Gabriel Celaya, and Blas de Otero.[5]

Perhaps the poet who has the most exhaustively explored the temporal and social themes in the contemporary manner is Gabriel Celaya, pseudonym for Rafael Múgica, whose work spans the years 1935 - 1969. A persistent Basque like Unamuno, Celaya has published almost forty books of poetry. Predictably he begins in the existential solitude of Unamuno and Machado, finding himself without roots and typically death-oriented; two early titles *Marea del silencio* (Tide of Silence) and *La soledad cerrada* (Closed Solitude) indicate this affiliation. But in *Música en la sangre* (Music in the Blood) his life-force drives him toward participation in life. In *Objetos poéticos* (Poetic Objects) he seeks to capture the fleeting splendor of things in lyrics he actually calls "poem-thing." In *Movimientos elementales* he returns to the reality of his corporal self, from which he reaches out toward God, a "God of wrath" who is "burning in the brambles." Finally he settles himself in life in *Tranquilamente hablando* (Tranquilly Speaking); in poems of marked colloquial tone he records the common daily experiences of his existence, an existence at times despairing, at times receptive to the simple beauties of things and people.

In *Las cartas boca arriba* (The Cards Face Upward), Celaya begins to move outside himself toward man in his social reality. Typically these "letters" are directed to contemporary, socially oriented poets such as Pablo Neruda and Blas de Otero. Like them, Celaya, now rejecting poetry as aesthetics, declares that it is "a weapon for transforming the world." Perhaps his outstanding poem in this manner is his intimate letter "To Andrés Basterra," which has already become an anthology piece. This humble Basque was an employee serving under Celaya in a company which handled timber from all parts of the world. The poem then becomes a paean to the values of work and the importance of human solidarity and communication. Celaya's *Cantos iberos* (Iberian Songs) amplify this theme to project a collective future for all Spain. In later years Celaya returns to the intimacy of himself and his Basque background. Finally, the poet yields to the preoccupations of the present day, jazz, modern physics, and wildly abstract painting. Gabriel Celaya has run the gamut of modern themes in an endless variety of contemporary forms.

For many the outstanding poet of this period is still another Basque, Blas de Otero, whose limited production effectively synthesizes the temporal and social themes.[6] In his first important book, *Angel fieramente humano* (Angel Fiercely Human), Otero plunges into his existential solitude in the manner of Unamuno, clawing in such desperation toward his lost God that God becomes a force destroying the poet, as the sonnet starkly entitled "Hombre" (Man) demonstrates:

> Alzo la mano, y tú me la cercenas.
> Abro los ojos: me los sajas vivos.
> Sed tengo, y sal se vuelven tus arenas.
>
> I lift my hand; at once you lop it off.
> I raise my eyes: you lash across them open.
> I thirst, and salt become your sands.

In these powerful sonnets, Otero, building upon the rough but forceful expression of Unamuno, achieves an original style characterized by short periods and carefully manipulated enjambment. In *Redoble de conciencia* (Drumroll of Conscience) the poet sinks even deeper into the morass of his own spiritual isolation; his "voice of the somber" becomes the voice of death, and he even pleads that God abandon him. Already in this book, however, there are signs that he is ready to turn to the reality of his human brothers in their common suffering.

One day in the early 1950s then, the poet who had "loved, lived, died within" destroyed all his former poems and went out in the street. In his *Pido la paz y la palabra* (I Ask for Peace and the Word), he directs his personal letter "To the Immense Majority," a direct challenge to Jiménez, who dedicated his poetry to what he called the "Immense Minority."

Yo doy todos mis versos por un hombre
en paz. Aquí tenéis, en carne y hueso,
mi última voluntad. Bilbao, a once
de abril, cincuenta y tantos. Blas de Otero.

I'll trade all my former verses for a man
In peace. Here I offer you, in flesh and blood,
My ultimate will. Bilbao, eleventh of April,
Nineteen-fifty something. Blas de Otero.

The poems of *I Ask for Peace and the Word*, in popular forms of essential but direct phrasing, express his cry for human solidarity, against the social injustice and oppression which was showing no letup in his country. He reiterates his faith in the power of the poetic word to transform his social dreams into a program of action in his next book *En castellano* (In Castilian), ultimately grounding himself in the potential of Spanish history and custom. Perhaps under the unremitting pressures and disappointments of his times, Blas de Otero has not yet succeeded in writing that final book which would establish his permanent place as the spokesman of his times.

Around 1963, in the ominous decade of the turbulent sixties, there began a significant change in the direction of Spanish poetry which has continued to develop to the present day.[7] When the rebellious youth in general finally responded to that line of poets from Machado through Alberti and Lorca to Celaya and Otero and took to the streets demanding human solidarity and social justice, a number of poets in the early sixties abandoned the social themes and turned in a new direction. While the minor figures especially have continued to express their tiresome weariness with a world grown thinner, bleaker, and utterly unpromising (the same world Jiménez found fresh and colorful and replete with vital symbols), the newer poets have seized upon the budding myths of the culture of the mass media. Among the poets of this new sensibility can be included Manuel Vázquez Montalbán, José María Alvàrez, Pedro Gimferrer, Ana María Moix, and Leopoldo María Panero.

Following the dictates of Marshall McLuhan, these newer poets exploit the themes and instant heroes of the mass media — the radio, the movies, the picture magazines, Rock music, Pop Art, the world of sport, and, above all, television. Since most of these media have become international, the newer poetry naturally has an international flavor. The poetry is sprinkled with the pop figures and tag phrases of our time: the comic figures such as Superman, lines from old movies, remembered phrases from popular songs. Woman is represented by movies stars of the immediate past, such as Yvonne de Carlo and Marilyn Monroe. The revolutionary hero is typically Che Guevara. Even for literary influences, the newer poets make a fetish of following international figures such as Octavio Paz, Eliot, Pound, St. John Perse, Kafka, Faulkner, etc. Of course, even the Generation of '98 pursued European influences, but generally assimilated them into a Spanish setting. However, the newer poets have apparently attempted to emphasize the shallowness of their Spanish culture by exalting their citizenship in the world.

In form, the newer poets have in general turned away from the common language and narrative patterns of the immediate past, for clarity and direct communication are no longer considered virtues. In fact, at times forms of collage are employed. Indeed, there is a recognizable link between the newer poetry and the various vanguard movements of the 1920s. Even the techniques of surrealism sometimes creep in; that is, the poet evokes a flow of free images supposedly from the subconscious which are transcribed deliberately without order and structure. In vocabulary the patterns oscillate between the commonest slang and the formal terms of literary criticism, since most of the poets have intellectual backgrounds. Typically these poets tend to exist in a private world with their kaleidoscopic images of the contemporary scene. From our present position it is of course impossible to predict if this new manner will produce a major poet.

Thus we come down to our present unsettled times, and (as has generally been the case) it seems that the possibilities for the poet and lyric poetry are bleak and discouraging. The major poets we have discussed have either passed on or have finished their careers. The poets now in maturity seem good but not great; among the younger poets no shining star has appeared to dazzle us with his genius by making poetry seem new and fresh and vital. Foreseeing this condition, Antonio Machado in his last years gloomily prophesied the disappearance of the lyric poet, arguing that in our times of mass media and depersonalization, individual sentiment would become superfluous and unappealing. For such times, Machado ironically predicted the invention of a mechanical hand-organ (fulfilled by the modern computer) to grind out the mass sentiments expected and appreciated. While we struggle to keep our faith against the evidence of Machado's prediction, at least we can draw strength from the achievements of the poets of the recent past in Spain. The poets of the Generation of '98 — Unamuno, Machado, and Jiménez — created their work under difficult social and political conditions, and the poets of the Generation of '27 — Lorca, Guillén, Aleixandre, Salinas, Diego, Alberti, Cernuda — managed to achieve theirs under the worsening conditions culminating in the Civil War. Surely it bears repeating that these major poets constitute a second Golden Age in Spanish poetry, and they have achieved a respected position in the literature of Western civilization.

Notes and References

Preface

1. Pedro Salinas, *Literatura española siglo XX* (México, 1949), pp. 34 ff.
2. Hugo Friedrich, *Estructura de la lírica moderna* (Barcelona, 1959), p. 228.
3. Federico de Onís, *Antología de la poesía española e hispanoamericana* (New York: Las Américas, 1961), p. xv.
4. Jiménez's mature ideas on modernism are found in Ricardo Gullón, *Conversaciones con Juan Ramón Jiménez* (Madrid: Taurus, 1958), and Juan Ramón Jiménez, *El modernismo* (Madrid, 1962).

Chapter One

1. The standard study of this movement is José López Morillas, *El Krausismo español* (México: Fondo de Cultura Económica, 1956).
2. Quoted in Guillermo Díaz-Plaja, *Modernismo frente a noventa y ocho* (Madrid, 1951), p. 3.
3. Ibid., p. 168.

Chapter Two

1. A solid biography in English of Unamuno is Margaret Thomas Rudd's *The Lone Heretic* (Austin: University of Texas Press, 1963). See also Martin Nozick's *Miguel de Unamuno* ([Boston] Twayne Publishers, 1971).
2. See Antonio Sánchez Barbudo, *Estudios sobre Unamuno y Machado* (Madrid: Guadarrama, 1959).
3. See Manuel García Blanco, *Don Miguel de Unamuno y sus poesías* (Salamanca, 1954).
4. This article is included in her *Poesía española contemporánea* (Madrid, 1961), pp. 91 - 170.
5. See Miguel de Unamuno, *The Christ of Velázquez*, trans. Eleanor L. Turnbull (New York, 1951), for a translation (faithful but not very poetic) of the complete poem.

147

Chapter Three

1. The first biography (somewhat deficient, to be sure) is Miguel Pérez Ferrero, *Vida de Antonio Machado y Manuel* (Buenos Aires: Espasa - Calpe, 1952). In English, see Alice Jane McVan, *Antonio Machado* (New York: The Hispanic Society, 1959), which also includes an anthology of translations.

2. We are closely following the structure of our *Antonio Machado* ([Boston] Twayne Publishers, 1971). Two fine general studies of Machado's poetry are those of Ramón de Zubiría, *La poesía de Antonio Machado* (Madrid, 1955) and of Segundo Serrano Poncela, *Antonio Machado, su mundo y su obra* (Buenos Aires: Losada, 1954).

3. Antonio Machado, *Obras, poesía y prosa*, ed. Guillermo de Torre (Buenos Aires, 1964), p. 48 (hereafter called *Obras*).

4. *Obras*, pp. 46 - 47.

5. We shall identify individual poems with the Roman numerals employed in *Obras*.

6. Ricardo Gullón, *Conversaciones con Juan Ramón Jiménez* (Madrid, 1958), p. 106.

7. See the long essay, "El pensamiento de Antonio Machado en relación con su poesía," in Antonio Sánchez Barbudo, *Estudios sobre Unamuno y Machado* (Madrid, 1959), which is a definitive study of Machado's metaphysical ideas.

8. *Obras*, p. 464.

Chapter Four

1. Quoted in *Historia general de las literaturas hispánicas*, ed. Guillermo Díaz-Plaja (Barcelona, 1967), VI, 381.

2. Ibid., p. 381.

3. Ibid., p. 382.

4. The most adequate biography of Jiménez is that of Graciela Palau de Nemes, *Vida y obra de Juan Ramón Jiménez* (Madrid: Aguilar, 1957).

5. Paul R. Olson, *Circle of Paradox. Time and Essence in the Poetry of Juan Ramón Jiménez* (Baltimore, 1967). This brilliant study treats Jiménez as a prototype of the modern poet.

6. We are identifying the poems quoted from the numbers in Jiménez's *Tercera antología poética* (Madrid, 1967). This anthology, in part at least selected by Jiménez himself, represents the work of the poet fairly adequately.

7. See Leo R. Cole's fine study, *The Religious Instinct in the Poetry of Juan Ramón Jiménez* (Oxford, 1967). See also Carlos del Saz-Orozco, *Desarrollo del concepto de Dios en el pensamiento religioso de Juan Ramón Jiménez* (Madrid: Editorial Razón y Fe, 1966), for a more biographical approach to Jiménez's religious struggles.

8. See, for example, the weak and malplaced article on Jiménez in *Historia general de las literaturas hispánicas*, VI, 337 - 86.

Chapter Five

1. See Luis Felipe Vivanco's fine chapter "La generación poética del 27" in *Historia general de las literaturas hispánicas* (Barcelona, 1967), VI, 463 - 578.

2. Quoted in Manuel Durán Gili, *El superrealismo en la poesía española contemporánea* (Mexico: Universidad Nacional, 1950), p. 30.

3. Salvador Dalí, *The Secret Life*, trans. Haakon Chevalier (New York: Dial Press, 1942), p. 176.

4. Luis Cernuda, *Estudios sobre poesía española contemporánea* (Madrid, 1957), p. 195.

5. Juan Ramón Jiménez, *Tercera antología poética* (Madrid, 1957), p. 1019.

6. Luis Felipe Vivanco, op. cit., p. 404.

Chapter Six

1. See Angel del Río, "Pedro Salinas. Vida y obra," *Revista hispánica moderna* 7 (1941), 1 - 32.

2. Pedro Salinas, *Poesías completas* (Madrid, 1955).

3. An unusually competent study of Salinas' poetry is that of Carlos Feal Deibe, *La poesía de Pedro Salinas* (Madrid, 1965). See also Julian Palley, *La luz no usada. La poesía de Pedro Salinas* (México: Andrea, 1966), and John Crispin, *Pedro Salinas* ([Boston] Twayne Publishers, 1974).

4. In the prologue of Pedro Salinas, *Poemas escogidos* (Buenos Aires: Espasa-Calpe, 1953).

5. It was published later in Pedro Salinas, *Volverse sombra* (Milano: Scheiwiller, 1957), pp. 25 - 32.

6. They were republished together by Clásicos Castalia (Madrid) in 1969 and defended as classics by the editor of the volume, Joaquín González Muela.

7. See Guillén's brief but helpful introduction to his work in Jorge Guillén, *Cántico, a Selection* (Boston, 1965).

8. This perceptive phrase is the title of the book which contains the papers delivered at the Guillén Conference in 1968: *Luminous Reality, The Poetry of Jorge Guillén* (Norman, Oklahoma: University of Oklahoma Press, 1969).

9. Julian Palley as translator has analyzed this poem in Jorge Guillén, *Affirmation, A Bilingual Anthology, 1919 - 1966* (Norman, Oklahoma: 1968), p. 185.

10. There is an excellent translation of this sonnet by Richard Wilbur in Jorge Guillén, *Cántico, a Selection*, p. 163.

11. See the biography of Antonio Gallego Morell, *Vida y poesía de Gerardo Diego* (Barcelona, 1956). A more "poetic" one is that of José Manrique de Lara, *Gerardo Diego* (Madrid: Ediciones y Publicaciones Españolas, 1970).

12. In the Preface of Gerardo Diego, *Primera antología de sus versos* (Buenos Aires, 1949), p. 19.

13. See the solid article on Diego's poetry by Dámaso Alonso in his *Poetas españoles contemporáneos* (Madrid, 1952), pp. 244 - 70.

14. There is a brief study of Diego's amorous poetry in José Manrique de Lara, op. cit., pp. 163 - 75.

15. See the poem "El encuentro" in *Poesía amorosa* (Madrid: Plaza y Janes, 1965), pp. 48 - 49.

Chapter Seven

1. See the long book by Ian Gibson, *The Death of Lorca* (Chicago, 1973).

2. We have summarized the details of Lorca's life in our book, *Federico García Lorca* ([Boston]: Twayne Publishers, 1967). The first frank biography of the poet is Jean L. Schonberg's *Federico García Lorca. L'homme. L'oeuvre* (Paris: Plon, 1956), which has been translated into Spanish. The most detailed biography is that of Fernando Vázquez Ocaña, *García Lorca. Vida, cántico y muerte* (Mexico: Biografías Gandesa, 1957).

3. In discussing Lorca's poetry we utilize our Twayne book. See also Gustavo Correa, *La poesía mítica de Federico García Lorca* (Madrid, 1970); Edwin Honig, *García Lorca* (New York: New Directions, 1944); and Roy Campbell, *Lorca: An Appreciation of his Poetry* (New Haven, 1959), in which Campbell translates significant sections from the ballads.

4. Francisco Umbral has developed this thesis in his *Lorca, poeta maldito* (Madrid, 1968).

5. It is included in the *Obras completas* (Madrid, 1967), p. 646.

6. As yet there is no biography of Alberti. His *La arboleda perdida, Libros primero y segundo de memorias* (Buenos Aires: Compañía General Fabril Editora, 1959), is a kind of poetic autobiography. The essential details of his life are given in the introduction to his *Poesías completas* (Buenos Aires, 1961).

7. The most complete study of Alberti's poetry (through *Sobre los ángeles)* is Solita Salinas de Marichal's *El mundo poético de Rafael Alberti* (Madrid, 1968). For the excellent short summary of his work in English, see the introduction by Luis Monguió in Rafael Alberti, *Selected Poems*, translated by Ben Belitt (Los Angeles, 1966).

8. Quoted in Rafael Alberti, *The Owl's Insomnia, Poems by Rafael Alberti*, trans. Mark Strand (New York, 1973), p. vii.

9. Carlos Bousoño, Aleixandre's major critic, developed this idea in his excellent prologue to Vicente Aleixandre's *Obras completas* (Madrid, 1960).

10. Although there is as yet no biography of Aleixandre (as he has wished it) Kessel Schwartz offers scattered biographical details in his book *Vicente Aleixandre* ([Boston]: Twayne Publishers, 1970). We gratefully acknowledge the general help received from this book.

11. See the chapter entitled "Freud, Surrealism and the Sea" in ibid., pp. 46 ff.

12. See Dámaso Alonso's meaningful articles on Aleixandre in his *Poetas españoles contemporáneos* (Madrid, 1952), pp. 281 - 332.

13. See Concha Zardoya's sensitive and profound articles on this and Aleixandre's other major books in her *Poesía española contemporánea* (Madrid, 1961), pp. 439 - 598.

s14. Vicente Aleixandre, *Mis mejores poemas* (Madrid: Gredos, 1961), p. 57. Aleixandre's own brief introductions to his books are helpful.

15. See Carlos Bousoño, *La poesía de Vicente Aleixandre* (Madrid, 1950). This definitive book is often too technical to be of much help to the general reader.

16. Vicente Aleixandre, *Poemas de la consumación* (Barcelona: Plaza y Janés, 1968). See the review of this book by José Luis Cano in *La poesía de la generación del 27* (Madrid, 1973), pp. 183 - 88.

17. Quoted from Luis Cernuda, *The Poetry of Luis Cernuda*, eds. Anthony Edkins and Derek Harris (New York, 1971), p. vii. This short essay is an excellent introduction to Cernuda's poetry; the anthology of translations is well selected and adequately translated. Cernuda's original text is found in Luis Cernuda, *Poesía y literatura* (Barcelona: Seix-Barral, 1960).

18. *The Poetry of Luis Cernuda*, p. vii.

19. See the fine study of Philip Silver, *"Et in Arcadia Ego." A Study of the Poetry of Luis Cernuda* (London, 1965).

20. See the fine discussion of this and other poems of Cernuda in Andrew P. Debicki, *Poesía española contemporánea* (Madrid, 1968), pp. 288 - 89.

Chapter Eight

1. In English, Charles David Ley's *Spanish Poetry Since 1939* (Washington, 1962) covers this period exactly. In Spanish see J. P. González Martín, *Poesía hispánica, 1939 - 1969 (Estudio y antología)* (Barcelona, 1970), and the excellent volume published in the United States by Gustavo Correa, *Poesía española del siglo veinte, Antología* (New York, 1972).

2. Hernández's poetry has been sensitively studied in Concha Zardoya's "Miguel Hernández: vida y obra," *Revista Hispánica Moderna* 21 (1954), 197 - 293.

3. See Andrew Debicki's competent book, *Dámaso Alonso* ([Boston]: Twayne Publishers, 1970).

4. Under the title *Children of Wrath*, Elias Rivers has published a translation of *Hijos de la ira* (New York: Johns Hopkins Press, 1970).

5. For a well-selected anthology of these poets, see Gustavo Correa, op. cit.

6. See Emilio Alarcos Llorach, *La poesía de Blas de Otero* (Salamanca: Anaya, 1961).

7. José María Castellet analyzes this period with distinction in the introduction to his *Nueve novísimos poetas españoles* (Barcelona, 1970).

Selected Bibliography

PRIMARY SOURCES

The poets discussed in this book are arranged alphabetically for editions of their works, including translations.

Rafael Alberti
Poesías completas. Buenos Aires: Losada, 1961.
Roma, peligro para caminantes. México: J Mortiz, 1968.
Selected Poems. Trans. by Ben Belitt. Berkeley: University of California Press, 1966.
The Owl's Insomnia; Poems. Trans. by Mark Strand. New York: Atheneum, 1973.
Concerning the Angels. Trans. by Geoffrey Connell. London: Rapp and Carroll, 1967.

Vicente Aleixandre
Obras completas. Madrid: Aguilar, 1968.

Luis Cernuda
La realidad y el deseo. México: Tezontle, 1958.
The Poetry of Luis Cernuda. Trans. by Anthony Edkins and Derek Harris. New York: New York University Press, 1971.

Gerardo Diego
Primera antología de sus versos. Madrid: Espasa Calpe, 1941
Segunda antología de sus versos. Madrid: Espasa Calpe, 1967.
Poesía amorosa. Barcelona: Plaza y Janés, 1965.

Federico García Lorca
Obras completas. Madrid: Aguilar, 1967.
The Gypsy Ballads. Trans. by Rolfe Humphries. Bloomington: Indiana University Press, 1953.
Lament for the Death of a Bullfighter and Other Poems. Trans. by A. L. Lloyd. London: Heinemann, 1937.

Poet in New York. Trans. by Ben Belitt. New York: Grove Press, 1955.
Selected Poems. Trans. by Donald M. Allen. Norfolk, Conn.: New Directions, 1961.

Jorge Guillén
Aire nuestro. Milano: Scheiwiller, 1968.
Cántico. Buenos Aires: Ed. Sudamericana, 1950.
Affirmation; a Bilingual Anthology. Trans. by Julian Palley. Norman: University of Oklahoma Press, 1968.
Cántico, A Selection. Trans. by Norman Thomas di Giovanni. London: André Deutsch, 1965.

Juan Ramón Jiménez
Libros de poesía. Madrid: Aguilar, 1957.
Primeros libros de poesía. Madrid: Aguilar, 1959.
Tercera antología poética. Madrid: Ed. Biblioteca Nueva, 1957.
Three Hundred Poems, 1903 - 1953. Trans. by Eloise Roach. Austin: University of Texas Press, n.d.

Antonio Machado
Obras, poesía y prosa. Buenos Aires: Losada, 1964
Poesías completas. Buenos Aires: Losada, 1962.
Eighty Poems of Antonio Machado. Trans. by Willis Barnstone. New York: Las Américas, 1959.

Pedro Salinas
Poesías completas. Madrid: Aguilar, 1961.
Truth of Two and Other Poems. Trans. by Eleanor L. Turnbull. Baltimore: Johns Hopkins Press, 1940.

Miguel de Unamuno
Obras completas. Vols. 13, 14, 15. Madrid: Aguado, 1958.
The Christ of Velázquez. Trans. by Eleanor L. Turnbull. Baltimore: The Johns Hopkins Press, 1951.
Poems. Trans. by Eleanor L. Turnbull. Baltimore: The Johns Hopkins Press, 1952.
The Last Poems of Miguel de Unamuno. Trans. by Edita Más López. Rutherford: Fairleigh Dickinson University Press, 1974.

SECONDARY SOURCES

1. Studies of Individual Authors
ALONSO, DÁMASO. "La poesía de Gerardo Diego." In *Poetas españoles contemporáneos.* Madrid: Gredos, 1965. This article emphasizes Diego's book *Lark of Truth.*

Bousoño, Carlos. *La poesía de Vicente Aleixandre.* Madrid: Gredos, 1968. The most complete study of Aleixandre's poetry, with special attention to the structural elements in it.

Campbell, Roy. *Lorca: An Appreciation of His Poetry.* New York: Haskell House, 1970. Includes many translations from the *Gypsy Ballads* by the poet Campbell.

Casalduero, Joaquín. *La poesía de Jorge Guillén.* Madrid: Suárez, 1953. One of the first important studies of Guillén's poetry.

Cobb, Carl W. *Federico García Lorca.* New York: Twayne Publishers, 1967.
————. *Antonio Machado.* New York: Twayne Publishers, 1971.

Cole, Leo R. *The Religious Instinct in the Poetry of Juan Ramón Jiménez.* Oxford: Dolphin Press, 1967. A deep study of the religious theme in Jiménez.

Coleman, Alexander. *Other Voices: A Study of the Late Poetry of Luis Cernuda.* Chapel Hill: University of North Carolina Press, 1969. A study of the use of the *persona* in Cernuda's poetry.

Correa, Gustavo. *La poesía mítica de Federico García Lorca.* Madrid: Gredos, 1970. A study of Lorca's poetry (especially the *Gypsy Ballads*) from the standpoint of myth.

Costa Viva, Olga. *Pedro Salinas frente a la realidad.* Madrid: Alfaguara, 1969. A general study of Salinas' poetry, following the poet's own critical guidelines.

Crispin, John. *Pedro Salinas.* [Boston]: Twayne Publishers, 1974. A competent study in which Crispin develops the "middle view" of Salinas as a "stoic realist."

Debicki, Andrew P. *La poesía de Jorge Guillén.* Madrid: Gredos, 1973. Well-written and well-organized study of this great poet.

Feal Deibe, Carlos. *La poesía de Pedro Salinas.* Madrid: Gredos, 1965. An outstanding study of Salinas' poetry, with emphasis upon stylistics.
————. *Eros y Lorca.* Barcelona: Edhasa, 1973. Exploration of a very complex subject in relation to Lorca.

Gallego Morell, Antonio. *Vida y poesía de Gerardo Diego.* Barcelona: Gredos, 1956. Important biographical details on Diego.

García Blanco, Manuel. *Don Miguel de Unamuno y sus poesías.* Salamanca: Universidad, 1954. One of the few books devoted to Unamuno's poetry only.

Gil de Biedma, Jaime. *Cántico: El mundo y la poesía de Jorge Guillén.* Barcelona: Seix-Barral, 1969. A sensitive study of Guillén by a contemporary poet.

González Lanuza, Eduardo. *Rafael Alberti.* Buenos Aires: Ediciones Culturales Argentinas, 1965. Includes biographical details and an anthology of Alberti's poetry.

Gullón, Ricardo. *Estudios sobre Juan Ramón Jiménez.* Buenos Aires: Losada, 1960. Mature articles on major aspects of Jiménez's poetry.

Ivask, Ivar and Juan Marichal, eds. *Luminous Reality. The Poetry of Jorge*

Guillén. Norman: University of Oklahoma Press, 1969. Short appreciative articles read at the conference devoted to Guillén.

Luis, Leopoldo de. *Vicente Aleixandre*. Madrid: Gredos, 1970.

Marías, Julián. *Miguel de Unamuno*. Trans. by Frances López-Morillas. Cambridge, Mass.: Harvard University Press, 1966. One of the essential books on Unamuno's ideas; one chapter sketches his poetry.

Marichal, Solita Salinas de. *El mundo poético de Rafael Alberti*. Madrid: Gredos, 1968. Very fine study of Alberti's poetry until 1929, including *Concerning the Angels*.

Nozick, Martin. *Miguel de Unamuno*. [Boston]: Twayne Publishers, 1971. This general study of Unamuno's work and ideas has one solid chapter on his poetry.

Olson, Paul R. *Circle of Paradox: Time and Essence in the Poetry of Juan Ramón Jiménez*. Baltimore: Johns Hopkins Press, 1967. Perhaps the outstanding single study of Jiménez's poetry.

Paz, Octavio. *Cuadrivio. Darío, López Velarde, Pessoa, Cernuda*. México: Ed. Mortiz, 1969. Fine general studies of Darío and Cernuda by this Mexican poet.

Sánchez Barbudo, Antonio. *Los poemas de Antonio Machado*. Barcelona: Lumen, 1967. A detailed study of Machado's poems, one by one.

Schwartz, Kessel. *Vicente Aleixandre*. [Boston]: Twayne Publishers, 1970. A very helpful introduction to Aleixandre's difficult poetry; limited biographical details.

Silver, Philip. *"Et in Arcadia ego": A Study of the Poetry of Luis Cernuda*. London: Tamesis, 1965. A masterful study of Cernuda's poetry as an expression of yearning for the classical Paradise.

Umbral, Francisco. *Lorca, poeta maldito*. Madrid: Biblioteca Nueva, 1968. Emphasis upon Lorca as a tragic, an "accursed" poet.

Vivanco, Luis F. "Rafael Alberti en su palabra acelerada y vestida de luces." In *Introducción a la poesía española contemporánea*, pp. 223 - 58. Madrid: Guadarrama, 1957. This article concentrates upon one of the salient aspects of Alberti's poetry.

Zubiría, Ramón de. *La poesía de Antonio Machado*. Madrid: Gredos, 1966. An excellent study of the essential themes of time and memory.

2. Studies of Contemporary Spanish Poetry

Alonso, Dámaso. *Poetas españoles contemporáneos*. Madrid: Gredos, 1965. Important source materials on Lorca's generation; articles written with a personal touch.

Bousoño, Carlos. *Teoría de la expresión poética*. Madrid: Gredos, 1970. One of the outstanding books of this century on poetic theory in Spain.

Bowra, Cecil M. *The Creative Experiment*. London: Macmillan & Co., 1949. Chapters devoted to Lorca and Alberti, among other European poets.

Cano, José Luis. *La poesía de la generación del 27*. Madrid: Guadarrama, 1970. A collection of Cano's articles and reviews.

CASTELLET, JOSÉ MARÍA. *Un cuarto de siglo de poesía española*. Barcelona: Seix Barral, 1966. An anthology (with a solid introduction) of poetry covering the years 1939 - 1964.

———. *Nueve novísimos*. Barcelona: Barral Editores, 1970. Important introduction to Spanish poetry since 1963, as well as an anthology.

CERNUDA, LUIS. *Estudios sobre poesía española contemporánea*. Madrid: Guadarrama, 1957. Important insights into modern Spanish poetry; very personal critical opinions.

COHEN, J. M. *Poetry of This Age (1908 - 1950)*. London: Arrow Books, 1960. One of the few studies of twentieth-century European poetry, with a fairly adequate presentation of Spanish poets.

CORREA, GUSTAVO. *Poesía española del siglo veinte*. New York: Appleton-Century-Crofts, 1972. An excellent anthology of the major twentieth-century Spanish poets, along with a reliable (though badly organized) introduction.

DEBICKI, ANDREW P. *Estudios sobre poesía española contemporánea*. Madrid: Gredos, 1968. Solid stylistic articles by this competent critic; good introductory chapter on the Generation of '27.

DÍAZ-PLAJA, GUILLERMO. *Modernismo frente a noventa y ocho*. Madrid: Espasa-Calpe, 1951. A controversial study of these two major movements.

FRIEDRICH, HUGO. *Estructura de la lírica moderna*. Trad. by Juan Petit. Barcelona: Seix-Barral, 1959. One of the most important books on European poetry since Baudelaire; Spanish poets receive generous treatment.

GRANJEL, Luis. *Panorama de la generación del 98*. Madrid: Guadarrama, 1959. A detailed historical study of the origins of the Generation of '98, along with appropriate texts from each member.

GONZÁLEZ MARTÍN, J. P. *Poesía hispánica, 1939 - 1969. Estudio y antología*. Barcelona: El Bardo, 1970. An excellent introduction to twentieth-century Spanish poetry; an anthology for the years indicated.

GONZÁLEZ MUELA, JOAQUÍN. *El lenguaje poético en la generación Guillén-Lorca*. Madrid: Insula, 1954. A technically competent study of poetic language in the Generation of '27.

GULLÓN, RICARDO. *Direcciones del modernismo*. Madrid: Gredos; 1963. A solid book by this competent scholar.

Historia general de las literaturas hispánicas. Vol. VI, *Literatura contemporánea*. Edited by Guillermo Díaz Plaja. Barcelona: Ed. Vergara, 1967. A massive history of Spanish literature; fine section on the Generation of '27.

ILIE, PAUL. *The Surrealist Mode in Spanish Literature*. Ann Arbor: University of Michigan Press, 1968. An analysis of the surrealist mode in Spain through studies of represenative figures — Lorca, Aleixandre, Dalí, Valle-Inclán.

JIMÉNEZ, JUAN RAMÓN. *El modernismo*. Madrid: Aguilar, 1962. Jiménez's personal (but mature) ideas on modern Spanish poetry, especially its origins.

Laín-Entralgo, Pedro. *La generación del noventa y ocho.* Buenos Aires: Espasa-Calpe, 1947. A study of the Generation of '98 according to essential themes.

Ley, Charles D. *Spanish Poetry Since 1939.* Washington: The Catholic University of America Press, 1962. Contains insights by the poets of this period into their own poetry; good bibliographies.

Morris, C. B. *A Generation of Spanish Poets, 1920 - 1936.* Cambridge: University Press, 1969. A study of the poets of the Generation of '27 according to selected themes.

Sáinz de Robles, Federico. *Historia y antología de la poesía española.* Madrid: Aguilar, 1964. An anthology containing a very extensive list of poets.

Salinas, Pedro. *Literatura española siglo XX.* México: Antigua Librería Robredo, 1949. Important short essays on the Generation of '98 and *modernismo.*

Siebenmann, Gustav. *Die moderne Lyrik in Spanien.* Stuttgart: W. Kohlhammer Verlag, 1965. A study of modern Spanish poetry according to essential themes.

Videla, Gloria. *El ultraísmo.* Madrid: Gredos, 1963. The standard study of this ephemeral movement in Spain.

Vivanco, Luis Felipe. *Introducción a la poesía española contemporánea.* Madrid: Guadarrama, 1957. Readable articles on almost all of the important twentieth-century Spanish poets.

Young, Howard T. *The Victorious Expression.* Madison: University of Wisconsin Press, 1964. Four general studies of the poetry of Unamuno, Machado, Jiménez, and Lorca.

Zardoya, Concha. *Poesía española contemporánea.* Madrid: Guadarrama, 1961. Excellent stylistic and thematic studies of modern Spanish poets, especially Jiménez and Aleixandre.

―――. *Poesía española del 98 y del 27.* Madrid: Gredos, 1968. Important articles on Unamuno, Alberti, and León Felipe, among others.

Index